INFERTILITY SUCCESS TO POSTPARTUM Mess

By

Erica Hoke
Raylene De Villiers, Mackenzie Fraser
Constance Lewis, Arielle Martone

With Foreword By:
Mandy Rodrigues, Clinical Psychologist

Copyright © 2023 Erica Hoke
1st Edition Copyright © Sarasota, Florida

ISBN 978-1-7375522-4-6
e-Book 978-1-7375522-5-3

All Rights Reserved

For Permissions email erica@ericahoke.com
No part of this book may be reproduced in any form or by any electronic or mechanical means, including information storage and retrieval systems, without written permission from the author, except for the use of brief quotations in a book review. All information shared in these chapters are the authors personal experiences and are not meant to treat, diagnose, or cure any illness or disease. Please consult your physician with any questions about procedures, tests or supplements mentioned here.

Editing by Melissa Denelsbeck
Cover Design: Meraki Cover Design

All information shared in these chapters are the authors personal experiences and are not meant to treat, diagnose, or cure any illness or disease. Please consult your physician with any questions about procedures, tests or supplements. The opinions expressed in this work are solely those of the individual authors and do not necessarily reflect the views of other authors, the publisher, or the editors.

CONTENTS

Title Page	1
Foreword Mandy Rodrigues, clinical psychologist	5
About Mandy Rodrigues	11
1. THE LIGHT AT THE END OF THE TUNNEL WAS A TRAIN Erica Hoke	13
About the Author	21
2. THE AFTERMATH Raylene De Villiers	23
About the Author	31
3. WHO IS THE WOMAN IN THE MIRROR Constance Lewis	33
About the Author	45
4. REBIRTH: TRANSCENDING POSTPARTUM DEPRESSION TO DISCOVER PURPOSE Arielle Martone	47
About the Author	63
5. HOW I THREW AWAY MY CRUTCHES Mackenzie Fraser	65
About the Author	77
Acknowledgement	79
BONUS CHAPTER FROM INFERTILITY SUCCESS, STORIES OF HELP AND HOPE FOR YOUR JOURNEY *Seven Diagnoses and Seven years to Four sons* Erica Hoke	81
Tell Us What You Think	93

FOREWORD

MANDY RODRIGUES, CLINICAL PSYCHOLOGIST

Many infertility survivors talk about an anticlimax both when they get pregnant and when they deliver. Those around them do not give these newly pregnant mothers the freedom to express distress with morning sickness, fatigue, and anxiety around each scan. Your day-to-day existence has been getting through the day – maybe for years. You continue throughout your pregnancy, anticipating the worst (the loss of your baby) and not imagining life beyond the pregnancy as you have learned to cope that way. It is too painful to imagine you will hold that baby in your arms. Let's face it; it hasn't been that way prior to this.

You feel guilty about not embracing your pregnancy and are bombarded with mothers enjoying their pregnancies and posting updates. You feel you should be grateful, elated, and glowing. You feel like an impostor. You likely walk on eggshells for nine months. It also seems that when you are faced with pregnancy after infertility, you feel somewhat robbed of the naivety of the pregnancy. You feel anxious for each ultrasound. At the beginning, you count the weeks, and then, you count the months to a healthy delivery. You are fearful of relaxing and enjoying the pregnancy as you are more consumed with what could go wrong.

Just because we are blessed with our baby, it doesn't mean we have no grounds to complain about the challenges of pregnancy and motherhood. For once, we want to be included and belong to our peer group of parents. We don't want our struggle to define us.

Most new mothers go through a period of baby blues after having their baby. This is a normal hormonal adjustment that happens a few days post-delivery. The biggest predictor of a post-natal depression is *pre-natal anxiety* and *depression*, and in your situation, you have the biggest risk factor but the least empathy. Many mothers who have struggled to conceive speak about feeling guilty that they cannot embrace their newborn baby as much as they thought they would. They desperately love their baby. But they feel they do not have the license to complain about sleepless nights, struggles with breastfeeding, and feeling down.

All mothers, through the ages, are expected to struggle with post-partum adjustment. Groups of women congregate around how this adjustment is challenging to themselves, their relationship, and the multiple roles they play. Post-natal depression is among the most underdiagnosed mental disorders of our modern time, and 40% of new mothers feel some sort of depression.

Mothers with histories of infertility have an even greater risk of developing postpartum depression, but they also have the most reluctance to talk about it, address it, or seek help. Fertility treatment should include counseling. However, this counseling should be given during the pregnancy as well as post-partum. ***The trauma of infertility extends beyond a positive test.***

The reaction to an infertility journey has been likened to the reaction to a chronic illness where you are not certain of the outcome. With a cancer diagnosis, for example, you might see a doctor who guarantees you a 95% survival rate if you follow the chemotherapy regimen. You put your life on hold and try to take it day by day. You feel awful, but you know that at the end of this, you have a 95% chance of going into remission. You have very little influence in your medical treatment as protocols are generally standard. You wait to ring that bell. That is your end goal. You wait to start your life again cancer-free. You get support along the way because there is more support with cancer. You are given empathy and leniency at work because everyone can visibly see your struggle. An illness like early-stage cancer is very traumatic.

Infertility does not have a prescribed treatment that guarantees some sort of success. There is no one-size-fits-all or universal protocol which, if followed correctly, will be successful. You go through the suggestions, the diet, the acupuncture, and the therapy, hoping that something will be successful. You might find you put your life on hold for months or years, only to look back empty handed.

A patient post-chemo and in remission stated that she always felt like she could not complain about anything less than another cancer diagnosis, as nothing was as bad as that. The same goes with infertility.

Most often, women with infertility struggle in silence, not able to bear the awkward conversations that come with including others in their experience. With infertility, there is never a guarantee of a positive outcome. People don't see your struggle. They don't understand your struggle. You can go through years of treatment and never get to ring that bell. You take it day by day, while trying to keep up with the other demands of your life. You no longer imagine a life without these struggles. You only focus on that positive result.

When you get that positive result, you are expected to be overjoyed and happy and stress-free. Society and those around you expect elation. However, infertility is likened to a trauma. When we are exposed to trauma, the reactions do not miraculously disappear when the trauma is over. When we are exposed to a robbery, it takes time to make sense of the incident and overcome the anxiety, the fear, and the intrusive thoughts.

A positive pregnancy result does not release or negate all the emotional baggage you have been carrying for months or years. It does not correct the potential damage caused to relationships or finances.

Going through infertility and succeeding with a pregnancy can still make us vulnerable to being anxious or depressed. We may have been so focused on the goal of getting pregnant that we have not allowed ourselves to imagine the future beyond the positive result. It was possibly too painful to imagine rubbing our pregnant belly or holding a baby in our arms. We think we will be **relaxed** and **happy**, but we have been through so much that we may be fearful of embracing our pregnancy. This is appropriate. It is not you being ungrateful. As we change, so do our mind maps. We have been avoiding pregnancy and baby-related triggers, and now is the time when they all come to the forefront. Our heart needs to catch up with our thinking brain.

And now, we have a squirming, screaming infant while we likely do not have our normal coping mechanisms available, and BOOM! The bomb goes off. It feels like the lid of the pot has come off, and all our vulnerabilities and insecurities come spilling out. The months, or possibly years, of anxiety and trauma have a way of sneaking up on us when we feel vulnerable. We ask ourselves, "Why now?"

We have our baby and have reached our goal, but suddenly, even the smallest tasks seem overwhelming. We might get tearful when our husbands leave for work or feel overwhelmed by just feeding ourselves. We might feel overly anxious about every cry or whimper from our baby. We feel isolated as we don't want to complain. We also feel we should be coping like all the other moms.

But we didn't start off with our glass full. We started with a deficit. We started with many months, or years, of not conceiving. We started off with a trauma, and when we have a trauma lurking in the background, it makes our coping skills less resilient. It also makes us more heightened to any form of stress – perceived or real. So, a crying baby that we cannot soothe coupled with trauma creates this perfect storm for anxiety or depression.

Having said that, the recognition of this temporary crisis can help us gain perspective. Making the storm predictable enables us to recruit resources to help us when we are most vulnerable. It is a sad reality that so many mothers are struggling but don't reach out for help. ***Instead, they wait for it to get easier and wonder how others do it.***

The first step is acknowledging that this will pass and that you are not alone. So many other mothers are going through the same, and when we are open about how we are feeling, we don't need to feel ashamed or like less of a mother. By sharing our stories, we are given hope that motherhood can be as beautiful as we anticipated. Sometimes, it takes a little support or a little change and a reminder that many others look back and wish they had spoken sooner.

ABOUT MANDY RODRIGUES

Clinical psychologist, Mandy Rodrigues, has worked in the field of infertility for the past 30 years. This has included working with individuals, couples and groups, helping them cope with the fertility journey and to make decisions as well as starting her career as a lecturer for WITS Medical School. She has been involved in forensic work since 2005 when surrogacy laws first came into place and was instrumental in developing guidelines for the High Court Applications. A large part of her practice involves stress management and the need for a multidisciplinary approach in infertility and Mandy has presented and published various books and articles on the subject. She is part of the groups House of Fertility, Empty Wombs and AngelBabiesSA as well as ambassador for myivfanswers, an international organization. She is on the board for SASREG and the Chairperson for the SIG Committee, representing counsellors in the fertility field in South Africa, as well as an ad-honorem member of the European Fertility Society. She has written numerous books as well as developed an online stress management course for women going through infertility, at www.tups.co. This has been presented internationally in a poster accepted for Eshre 2007, evaluating the efficacy of the time to pregnancy in these women. She has contributed a chapter for a medical textbook in the UK, and is part of the BIOLAWGIC Committee creating guidelines for surrogacy, gamete assessments and especially the new laws surrounding known donors. She is involved in staff training for miscarriage, loss and neonatal counselling.

1

THE LIGHT AT THE END OF THE TUNNEL WAS A TRAIN

ERICA HOKE

Someone once said that infertility is like walking along a dark tunnel that you never know is going to end (with a living child). If infertility is the tunnel, then motherhood after infertility is the train. No one tells you the joke is on you and that the light isn't a peaceful, blissful end to your journey but that the train is coming to run you over.

I know this to be true now, but I wouldn't ever have admitted this after the birth of my first son. I was so caught up in others' expectations to "bounce back" that I fell right into our "normal" routine at home. I came home from the hospital, and although I'm not 100% sure, I think I cooked dinner that night (or the next) for my husband and my in-laws, who stayed with us for the first 6-weeks after our son was born. What I'm saying is that after a multi-day long delivery and hospital stay, I felt great, *and* someone should have been taking care of me other than me.

To be honest, I felt selfish after our infertility journey to demand privacy and space. I was a *new* breastfeeding mom, after all. My husband is an only child, and my in-laws expected that this would be their only grandchild. I might as well have given birth to the Messiah. Breastfeeding was going great, but I was still self-conscious. Self-conscious yes, that was part of it, but breastfeeding also was my excuse to steal away and be alone with our son. It was a respite from not being comfortable in my own home. While I was happy to be alone, I became increasingly lonelier. My husband seldom joined me, and I felt super isolated since newborns feed almost non-stop.

Tip: After birth, be true to yourself, even if it means hurting people's feelings. Even though my husband and I agreed that six weeks was too long for his parents to visit and stay with us, we didn't stand up to them. I strongly encourage you to protect your time with your new baby and limit visitors for the first few weeks while you're healing, your hormones are settling, and you're getting used to being a mother. Especially if it's your first child, find ways your family can support you that are truly helpful and you're both comfortable with.

The extended visit colored everything. I had no concept of how quickly my baby would grow, and later, I felt cheated of the time my husband and I missed out on just sitting on the couch as a couple and getting to know our new son. It only surfaced when we got our privacy back.

I'll never forget when we invited some friends over. My feelings boiled over after six weeks of growing increasingly frustrated at not being seen and my needs not being met. We were having a great time chatting and passing the baby around when it was time for a feed. I excused myself, and he and I settled into the nursery to feed. I heard the slider open and close, and my husband moved the dog into the house. He was a barker and it was obvious he did not like being separated from the people he could see outside. Bark, he did. Great! I thought, now I'm stuck in the house with a barking dog! I tried but couldn't get my husband's attention. I fumed. Finally, I got up and angrily flung the slider open, letting him know that I didn't appreciate being trapped in the house with a barking dog. Our friends left soon after. Yes, it was my choice to breastfeed, and we were also in a situation where our son would not, under any circumstance, take a bottle of any kind. So I was left as the sole source of food, and that was harder than I was willing to admit.

The pressure of hosting family that left me feeling isolated, along with my growing anxiety surrounding taking care of our son, set me up for a perfect storm of postpartum anxiety. At my doctor's check-up I nodded that I was fine when they asked if I was having any postpartum issues. I didn't want to admit it to them because I would do *nothing* to jeopardize my postpartum journey, and I didn't want to admit it to myself because I felt so much pressure to "keep it together." I wouldn't allow myself to complain about this easy-going son we had prayed and wished and longed for.

If my anger flared with my husband, my anxiety showed itself at my breastfeeding support group. It was my lifeline to feeling connected at a time when I wanted reassurance that my son's behavior was normal and that the breastfeeding was going well. One day, as a group, we had just come from a pediatrician's well-baby check-up. My son had a rash on his face, and I was really anxious about it. In talking to the group leader, she assured me he was fine. I breathed a sigh of relief and burst into tears. "I feel like everything and anything is going to kill him!" I exclaimed. Ahh, there it was, the source of all my anxiety.

Tip: Don't "sugar-coat" your mental health to your partner. Even if you don't fully understand why you're feeling the way you do, be sure to share it. And check in with them, too. Having a new baby changes everything about your life. Don't pretend it doesn't, or avoid the conversations.

Did I mention that despite all this angst and anxiety, our son was a dream baby? Whatever the book said, we did, and he followed. He slept, nursed, and pooped like he was running a train schedule according to his biological clock. I think we thought we were geniuses. So much so that we decided to "try again," which is ridiculous enough since we had just been through an infertility journey. He was 15 months old and we knew that we wanted siblings for him. After having some hormone levels tested, the results were no surprise and not great, but even so, I reluctantly gave up breastfeeding for a chance at a sibling for him.

We went to another reproductive medicine doctor for a second opinion on my lab results. It turns out that he didn't disagree with our original doctor, but he did feel like I should have some blood thinner prescription available since I have factor 5 Leiden. This blood clotting disorder can cause miscarriage or loss at any stage of pregnancy. The medication would allow me to start treatment at the first sign of pregnancy and potentially prevent a loss. That appointment was on a Tuesday. On Friday, I realized that my cycle should have started, and I decided to take an at-home pregnancy test. It was positive. I was in shock and overjoyed! I filled my prescription and called my OB/GYN.

From the beginning of the pregnancy, it felt different. My husband noticed I didn't say "the baby" but rather "the babies." Wait! What? I guess I was having premonitions about having twins. We would have to wait until our eight-week appointment to find out. The wait was torture. Our office was super busy on the day of our appointment. They told us it could be hours. We settled in and waited. We weren't going home without seeing our baby/babies. Once it was our turn, the doctor hurriedly told us he only had one healthy baby! We left the office excited but skeptical.

Happily, we went on vacation. And then I got sick. Really sick. Morning sickness, along with a hacking dry cough. I coughed and coughed and coughed. I couldn't sleep, I couldn't eat, what I did eat didn't stay down. I was miserable. By the time we arrived home from vacation, I had already booked an appointment with my OB/GYN. My son also caught a cold, so my husband stayed behind to look after him. In addition to getting me some medication for my cough, my doctor also wanted to take a look at the baby. It was the last appointment of the day. I'll never forget the moment the doctor placed the ultrasound wand on my stomach and I saw the screen light up with what appeared to be two fried eggs in a skillet. I immediately exclaimed, "That looks like two babies!" And so it was. I was pregnant with twins! After years of infertility and being told I would need donor eggs to conceive, my second pregnancy at 39 was a set of twins.

Despite a seemingly endless amount of doctor appointments, I would learn that the easiest thing about mothering twins was being pregnant with twins. I was very closely monitored due to my age and underlying health issues, but other than that, I had a dreamy twin pregnancy. My three biggest anxieties were that I wouldn't be able to tell them apart, they would need NICU care, or that I would end up with a c-section. We would have to see about the first concern, but it didn't look good for a double vaginal delivery since one of the babies was transverse, lying across the top of my stomach. We could only wait and see if he flipped to head down position after baby A was delivered.

TIP: It's my opinion that having autonomy in your birthing decisions helps you feel better about the outcome, whatever it may be. Everyone thought I was crazy to risk a vaginal birth and a c-section, but being forced into a c-section because both babies weren't head down would have caused me to feel let down about the whole birth experience. I needed to walk that out and take that chance for myself. So much of an infertility journey is someone in the medical community telling you what to do. These birth choices help restore your power over your body. The outcome goal should be a healthy baby AND a healthy mom, both mentally and physically.

When I agreed to my induction at 39 weeks, my body was already in a labor pattern. We waited and labored without much progress for most of the day and overnight. Even though I was given Pitocin, my labor was not progressing. After almost 20 hours in labor, I decided to let the doctor break my water. My labor went from a meandering river to class 5 rapids within minutes. Within 90 minutes, I was fully dilated and ready to push, with only one minor issue…the epidural. It was hospital policy to have the epidural in place and deliver in an operating room designated for multiple birth pregnancies. My labor had progressed so quickly that it caught everyone off guard. After several attempts, the anesthesiologist got the epidural in place. Off to the OR they wheeled me; all the while I could feel baby "A" crowning. Once in the OR, in dramatic fashion, my doctor burst through the doors, hands dripping, got into position, and when I pushed with the next contraction, baby "A" was delivered! He then turned his attention to baby "B" and found his umbilical cord wrapped tightly around his body, and it was short. After the doctor attempted to unwind him he determined it was causing too much distress. On top of that my cervix was closing and I would have a second labor. Time for Plan B. I was having a c-section.

If my post op, postpartum care was any indication of how the whole twin thing was going to go, I was in trouble. Just a short time after getting settled in my room with my TWO babies and still reeling from the huge amount of anesthesia, I was bombarded by nurses wanting my attention to fill out paperwork and sign this or that. The patient. Who had just given birth vaginally and by c-section. It was too much. I distinctly remember holding *both* babies in a chair, already feeling like I might drop one any minute, vomiting into an emesis bag, and filling out paperwork with the nurse. She couldn't have cared less. No one offered to take one of the babies from me.

TIP: As in labor and birth, you must advocate for your patient experience. I wish I had kindly told that nurse that I would not be filling out any paperwork until the next day.

And so it went. Apparently, I had done such a good job looking capable and taking care of everything that no one doubted I would rise to the occasion and be just fine with a two-year-old and two newborns that I was breastfeeding. I was not okay. My in-laws were staying with us again, but for a shorter time, my sister came for a few days but had to return to her family, and my mom came too. I had a houseful of people but very little help. My older son was entertained, they helped with some of the cleaning, and I tried my best to keep up with the cooking for us all. My husband took a week off of work. Everyone I met who knew my situation always enthusiastically said to me, "But you had help, right?" Um, no, NO, I didn't. To say I was exhausted doesn't even come close to touching how depleted I was. I distinctly remember the day my sister left for the airport. I practically grabbed her by the ankle to prevent her departure. I have never felt so alone in my life.

Make no mistake, my husband was right there in the trenches with me. He got up for night feeds and changed and swapped babies with me until we figured out how to manage them both at one time. I was starving all the time and always needed water when I sat down to nurse and never seemed to have it. Once again, the breastfeeding went fairly smoothly, probably better than most people's experience, however, the twins had escaped the NICU, but they were sooooo tiny! This meant LOTS of frequent feeding. One had jaundice, and the other lost more than 10% of his body weight. I was desperate to keep formula away from my babies. I called on my friend, who was a twin mom and lactation consultant. She helped me maximize their feeds and taught me how to tandem feed. Things got better and then worse. Worse because they *just* nursed. They wanted me and me only. After my first son refused a bottle and I had to return to work, I was super determined not to fall into the same trap. We started early and in earnest to give them a bottle. I was producing enough for them but got very little pumping, which created a huge problem. The frustration of an extra "feed/pumping" with so little results was not encouraging. Still, we persisted and tried feeding methods other than a bottle, such as a soft feeding spoon and some other devices the lactation consultant brought from the hospital for us to try. Nothing worked. For the first year, I could only leave the house for an hour and a half at a time before they needed me. The mental pressure was exhausting.

> *Tip: Set up help before you give birth. Do whatever you have to do (refinance your house, borrow money, find a church group to help you, find a tween on your block who can be another set of hands for you, etc.) to create a space where YOU, the MOTHER, are taken care of. I strongly recommend looking into a postpartum doula or other mother care. Make accommodations for siblings, which means a preschool or in-home help. If*

> *you are having multiples, it's not reasonable to think you will be able to care for several babies and a toddler.*

Fueled by my severe lack of sleep, my depression spiraled. I always said back then that having twins was the loss of convenience. Even if I didn't have my two-year-old with me, I still couldn't just pop into the store for milk or bread, toting one of those heavy car seats on each arm. Everything was a PRODUCTION. Even trips to a music class at the library nearly required rocket science technology to execute. It just wasn't worth it. It was the perfect storm of isolation.

Finally, my experienced twin mom/lactation consultant was the one who recognized I was drowning. She had encouraged me early on to get help with my older son, and I refused, thinking I would traumatize him by putting him in a preschool so soon after the arrival of his baby brothers. I was wrong. When the twins were six months old, that's exactly what I did. He was closer to two than three, and it broke my heart, but it was necessary. I just couldn't keep up with everyone's needs.

Preschool was the first thing I did to start taking care of my own needs. Then, again at her suggestion, I found a tween down the street who would work for a few dollars an hour, helping me after dinner/during bedtime when my husband traveled for business. Eventually, when the twins were eating solids and not so dependent on me, I found a women's bible study that offered childcare. It was my first study ever, and it became a lifeline for me. Little by little, as we passed the first year, the pressure eased, but I will never forget the intense feelings that first year produced. If you ever want to know how living every minute of every hour around the clock feels, ask a twin mom.

Now, when I see twin strollers out in public, I make sure that I look that woman straight in the eye and let her know that I see her, that keeping two babies alive is hard, and that she's going to make it too. And if they're past a year, I will say, "Good job! You made it past the first year! And everyone is still alive!" I've never had anyone shrug that off; it's universal.

ABOUT THE AUTHOR

Erica Hoke wears many hats but the one she is most proud of is Mom. She is an Infertility Strategist, a prolific Author, and a dedicated Publisher. But at her core, she is a woman who has walked the rocky path of infertility and emerged victorious. Her life's mission, born out of personal experience, is to empower other women battling the same.

A bleak diagnosis once painted Erica's future with less than a 1% chance of natural conception. Rejecting the conventional all-or-nothing approach, Erica embarked on a journey less traveled. She sought alternative methods, delved deep into research, and pursued relentlessly until she uncovered the root cause of her fertility issues. She is the proud mother of four beautiful children, each one a testament to her unwavering determination and resilience.

But Erica's story isn't exclusive. It is a reflection of thousands of women who, like her, have successfully unearthed the root causes of their fertility issues. Through her work, she hopes to light the way for those still navigating the challenging terrain of infertility. Because, as Erica knows all too well, it's not about the destination, but the journey that shapes us.

2

THE AFTERMATH

RAYLENE DE VILLIERS

This chapter may be uncomfortable to read or trigger you. You may potentially not understand, but this is my truth, my feelings, and my thoughts, so unless you have walked in my shoes, I ask you not to judge me. I backed out of this book twice due to the sheer trauma of having to relive this again many years down the line.

My triplet daughters turn into teenagers this year, and still, it hurts to go back in time and examine my thoughts, actions, and behaviour. I need to process the aftermath of years of infertility, having a stressful triplet pregnancy, raising triplets plus one, and going from a family of two to six within the space of two years.

There simply is not a medical professional who specializes in, or even understands, the deep, soul-destroying trauma that most, if not all, infertility patients have to endure to have their children. The trauma is physical on our bodies, it is spiritual as we seek answers, it is financial on our wallets, it is emotional with our partners, and it is pure devastation when the treatment is not successful. But once you have received a positive pregnancy test, you are meant to go forth and be happy. That is far from the truth. All is not always well that ends well.

My story of conception and birth can be found in the previous book titled "Infertility Success: More stories of help and hope for your journey" chapter "By the Moon and the Stars." The following part of my story takes place after my triplets plus one were born. I conceived twice and birthed four children in the space of 26 months.

Your positive pregnancy test is the start; next comes the baby and the baby carriage, and then, the post-traumatic stress syndrome from the years of infertility. Let me explain what that looks like in my world.

I cannot have anyone else pick my children up from school. I cannot trust another human being (including my husband) to pick them up from school. I worry he will get the time wrong and the place wrong. There are small things that keep coming up that remind me that I am still not over infertility or its insidious torments. The thought of losing any of my children sends me into a depression so vast and so deep that I feel sure I wouldn't return; in fact, I know I wouldn't.

I used to call it survival mode, but the real identity of survival mode is post-traumatic stress syndrome (PTSD), and it's taken me ten years to figure out that this is what I am suffering from. PTSD is defined as *"the development of stress symptoms following a traumatic event or several traumatic events."* It's exposure to traumatic events over a period of time and dealing with the aftermath of these events.

I have PTSD due to my years of failed fertility treatments and my miscarriage at 8 weeks after IVF number 2. It was five very long years, a LOT of money, and the devotion of a good percentage of my life in my late 20s to researching the ultimate winning combination to succeed in becoming a mother. PTSD almost never exists without her friends – shame, guilt, anxiety, and depression. This period of my life left me with an addiction to antidepressants and anti-anxiety medication that took me six months to finally wean off of, 15 years after starting them. Medical doctors are ultra-fast in prescribing high schedule addictive medication to women who have been emotionally beaten down by the medical fraternity.

> *TIP: Before starting on any kind of antidepressant or anti-anxiety medication, make sure you understand they are seriously addictive and have withdrawal symptoms associated with*

high schedule drugs. Think twice before starting down this path.

If you want to know what PTSD after infertility looks like, here's an example. I've been a mother for eleven years, but still, the reminders of a normal pregnancy stings to the point of tears. I'd just returned home from a social event. I knew some of the ladies, but most, I'd never met, which I was already freaking out about. I sashayed up to two ladies chatting. I felt totally out of my depth, but I persisted. We'd been in the midst of a pandemic for close to two years, so I understood my social skills were probably worse than ever. From the conversation, I gathered they are both pregnant (typical). I tried my best to add to their conversation; I even told them that I had the same heartburn and cravings (which I didn't, I just wanted to be part of the conversation). I ended up making an excuse to use the bathroom because to this day, I have PTSD about pregnancy, other women becoming pregnant, or anything remotely pregnancy related. I still mute friends who fall pregnant on social media so I can avoid seeing their black and white sonar photos. How ridiculous is that? To this day, I cannot rub another woman's pregnant tummy or even have much joy in a pregnancy announcement. It is just too much for me to think about or even acknowledge. Eleven years, and I still have the same response – deflect, ignore, pretend.

> *TIP: Be honest with your friends and family. Tell them you are struggling and won't be attending family events with children. It's okay to be honest and protect yourself.*

I never imagined that becoming a mother would be so difficult – both the act of getting pregnant, which I failed miserably at, and then the actual "being a mom" part. You know that image you have in your mind way before you ever conceive – a new mother slowly and gently rocking their beautiful newborn baby in a rocking chair, gently soothing them into slumber whilst you stare into their cute face? It sounds delightful, and I wanted that; from as early as five years old, I wanted to be a mommy. Once we knew we were going to have triplets, I realized that life would be a little insane. To be honest, having multiples as your first "baby" robs you of that special bond most mothers of singletons get to experience. I don't have one single photo of me with all three of my girls. I never rocked or held any of my children to sleep, and I didn't spend much time with them at all, especially in the first year of their lives. It was a sausage factory in our house. Feed, swaddle, nap, feed, swaddle, nap, feed, swaddle, nap–every three hours on repeat for m-o-n-t-h-s.

I was one, and there were three of them. One versus three. The three won over me almost every day. My husband would come home after work some days and would not know or understand what to do with us. It would be three babies and an adult crying, except the adult was barely able to function. We don't live close to our immediate family, so we had one nanny to help us during the day, and we did night shift together. Even if we could have afforded a night nurse, I would never have allowed someone in my house to look after my children whilst I slept. I imagined her stealing them in the middle of the night and me waking up to empty cots in the morning. Again, PTSD and her best friend, anxiety, appeared and caused irrational thoughts.

TIP: Get help, and then, allow that help to help you!

A dichotomy exists in most mothers who have been through the IVF process, wanting to have a baby so, so very much, and then, oftentimes, once you are on the other side and have reached motherhood, you wonder what on earth you just did. What you imagined it would be like and what it actually is like can be a bit different and horrific and you stare down this barrel of reality.

In South Africa, you *may* have a discussion on your "mental health" with your gynecologist at your 6-week postpartum appointment. It normally comes straight after which contraceptive you would like to use going forward. The mental health question is fleeting, maybe lasting less than a minute for you to summarize what you are experiencing in your head at that moment in time, and most responses (including mine) was "it's going okay."

Meanwhile, back at home, you are close to going down the rabbit hole of insanity, but you feel like you can't really express your true feelings because you should feel LUCKY for being an IVF success story. You know your IVF friends are still in the trenches looking at you hopefully, or you see the friend you asked to stop messaging you her sonar pictures a few years back, and now it is impossible to connect with her, even though you are both mothers now. You are judged by the decisions you made back then to protect your heart from infertility and the lack of a baby in your arms, and now that your baby is in your arms, you are judged by your actions of not being entirely ecstatic about motherhood. There seems to be no winning scenario.

One morning, the girls woke up (as usual) around 4:30 for their feed, but this time, they refused to sleep again. I remember sitting outside our house on the grass with my husband as the sun was rising and the birds chirping, listening to babies screaming their lungs out whilst I sobbed. I grabbed the car keys and jumped in my car, still in my pajamas, and started driving. I wanted to drive as far away as possible from the manic chaos that was my house at that moment. I drove for a long time, just thinking, trying to understand why I wanted to get away from the life I had wanted for so long, prayed for, manifested, and conjured my family. I had begged God at one stage to please send me a child or take me out of this universe. I wanted to give up my own life if a baby was not meant to be part of it, and now, here I was driving away from them.

I hadn't been able to process the trauma of infertility, seven IVFs, a miscarriage, a positive conception, a very difficult pregnancy, pre-eclampsia, NICU time, expressing breastmilk, the guilt of no longer expressing breastmilk ... the list goes on at infinitum.

Then, I felt a shift happen. The girls were five, turning six years old, and my son was three years old. I felt like I had been in survival mode for five years. The children were becoming a bit more self-sufficient and didn't need me as much as they did when they were babies or toddlers. My husband and I had started to drift apart, not due to anything that happened, but we called it "ships passing in the night." Once the children were sorted and in bed, we were both exhausted and would go to bed early. It became a hamster wheel of wake up, entertain, feed, and bathe children, go to bed, and repeat.

I started getting anxious. Is this what the rest of my life would be like? I was bored and suffering from major depression and probably in the numbing or fawning phase of my PTSD. I had lost ME. I had no idea who I was any longer; I didn't even know what I liked to do. I went to see a psychologist who told me I needed time alone and to do something I enjoyed. I didn't even know where to start. I was a mom and wife living on a hamster's wheel.

This has been the most difficult part of this journey; I did many a stupid thing in trying to find ME again. I went out with friends, drinking heavily, moving further apart from my husband, and even missing out on time at home with my children whom I had wanted so much. This led me into further guilt and depression. I didn't even know if this was the life that I wanted any more.

I started becoming more esoteric, learning to read runes and tarot cards to help me find answers. I saw many counselors, life coaches, and psychologists, but none helped. I changed my medication, but I still felt this hollow, dark, deep unhappiness. Why was I this unhappy when I finally had the picture-perfect family? Because it's fucking hard being a mother to four children, together with what I see now was infertility-based PTSD. I felt like I failed to get pregnant, and now, I was failing at being a mother. I kept reminding myself of that time I drove away from my children and how I promised I would never do that again, but yet, that is all I wanted to do – run the fuck away.

The denial or numbing stage of PTSD is a well-known step in trying to protect or numb yourself from the events that occurred. Avoiding difficult emotions through denial is the mind's way of ensuring it isn't hurt any further by eliminating the high stress and anxiety it is feeling. ***People suffering PTSD need to deal with this stage to enable their mind to move forward.*** This is the stage I was stuck on for years.

The present time is what I would like to think of as my rescue and recovery phase of my infertility PTSD. I've started to come to terms with what I had to endure to have children. I've had to learn to dig deep into my soul to forgive myself, to let go of the shame and show my vulnerability.

Brene Brown (although she doesn't know I exist) saved me from myself. I've listened to and watched everything she has produced and consider her a huge influence in my life. She is an incredible motivational speaker, and I used to listen to her audible books in between driving to clients, running errands, grocery shopping, and extra murals, and this helped me immensely. Her most powerful quote of all times is, **"Daring greatly means the courage to be vulnerable. It means showing up and being seen. To ask for what you need. To talk about how you're feeling. To have the hard conversations." – Brene Brown**

TIP: PTSD recovery does not need to be in a psychologists consulting room. To be able to process, I needed to feel the emotions. That's the hard part. I threw lots of money at therapy, but without doing the hard part myself of feeling feelings, I was not able to move past the trauma.

I may not have the answers. I still need to do a lot of work on myself and purposefully try to do so daily. When that wave of depression or anxiety hits me, I've learnt to roll with it. Keep that feeling; don't dismiss it because it WILL pass. Allow the feelings to exist within you because wishing them away means they will only return and probably be worse than before.

If I had to do things over, would I do the same? Yes, 100% I would. My children are my everything, and to have missed out on meeting them would have been the biggest travesty. They make me insane but also keep me sane and keep me here. I would have lived an extravagant life without them – a lonely extravagant life. They make me who I am today. Without them, I'd be a smaller version of myself, BUT it's not easy. I love them with every fiber of my being, and soon, hopefully, I'll love myself again.

Infertility robs you of normalcy; it rapes you whilst you are awake. I don't wish infertility on my very worst enemy because nobody should struggle to have a child they are so desperately ready for. My heart goes out to anyone still struggling; may the universe provide for you and set you free from your shame.

ABOUT THE AUTHOR

Raylene is mom to four beautiful children – triplet girls and a son. The road to becoming parents was not an easy one for Raylene and her husband; the part about leaving contraceptives and getting pregnant the next month was a fairytale not to be seen for them. After what felt like a lifetime of doctor visits, tests, injections, and pure determination, Raylene finally birthed her triplets. The story is not the traditional one, but if it helps just one other person reading this book, then it was all worth it.

"Everything will be okay in the end. If it's not okay, it's not the end"

~ John Lennon

3

WHO IS THE WOMAN IN THE MIRROR

CONSTANCE LEWIS

Infertility, for me, was a long and hard 6-year journey filled with loss. I thought about all the pain we experienced and expected it would disappear when my first child was born. I thought that his birth alone would heal me. I expected it would be the happiest I had ever been. After all I had been through, I was finally at the finish line. The reward was my newborn baby.

When that healing didn't happen, I was shocked. My dream of being a mother had come true. Why did I not feel overwhelming happiness? I didn't recognize the person who looked back at me in the mirror. I had lost my identity completely. I looked into her tear-filled eyes and felt ashamed of her. She was not the mother I thought she would or should be.

My lowest point brought me to the realization that I needed help. I knew I would never be the same person I was before. I was a different me but someone I found to love again. It was not an easy journey. I worked hard using many at-home techniques, cognitive behavior therapy, medicine and non-medicine treatments. I reached out to my community and support system when I needed it. Because of the work I put in after my first child, the postpartum anxiety/depression was less with my second and third child.

. . .

TIP: Make sure to heal your past wounds. PTSD or other emotional issues from your fertility, infertility, and/or experiences can and will affect your postpartum journey in a negative way.

My infertility journey impacted my postpartum journey significantly. I had experienced so much loss at that point, with miscarriages and many disappointments. Even during my pregnancy, I had severe anxiety. I was worried about loss constantly. I was always checking for blood each time I used the restroom. It was hard for me to enjoy the pregnancy and feel connected to my baby. I remember feeling guilty for not wanting to bond with my baby while I was growing him. Other women seemed so happy to be pregnant – always talking to their baby and rubbing their bellies. I don't remember being able to relax and do this. I kept telling myself I would feel so much better when he was here and healthy.

When my son was born, I expected the fear of loss to stop. However, the moment Miles came into this world, I felt a different kind of fear. I loved him unconditionally and knew I would be his protector forever. I knew most parents felt this way. The normal maternal instinct to keep your offspring safe is ingrained into our DNA. So, I thought this is a normal feeling.

This intense feeling grew each day over the next few months. It became unhealthy, and at the time, I did not recognize the severity of it. As a women's health nurse practitioner, I see postpartum anxiety and depression on a daily basis. I'm able to recognize it and treat it. I help so many women every year feel better and find their way out of that dark place. But I was unable to see it in myself. I thought it was normal to feel this scared and anxious as a new mother.

I wish I had known to treat my PTSD and emotional trauma with infertility before I delivered my son. I did not realize the significant impact that it would have. I know my postpartum anxiety and depression was worse because of my past experiences.

After we got home from the hospital, the first weeks were a blur. I remember taking him to the pediatrician multiple times because he lost so much weight, and I refused to supplement. I wanted him to get my breast milk only. Although the pediatrician was great and didn't pressure me, I felt like I wasn't able to feed my baby enough. I remember trying to put him on a schedule early – breast-feeding every 2 1/2 to 3 hours instead of just letting him feed on demand. I also had to wear a nipple shield because I had problems with latch, and this impacted my milk supply as well. He was a skinny little baby, and that worried me. I remember having a friend who had a baby at the exact same time as me, and her baby was already sleeping for at least 5 hour stretches. My baby was still waking up every 2 to 3 hours. I thought for sure this meant I wasn't doing a good job, that he was hungry.

Tip: If you find yourself obsessing about the baby's weight, talk to your pediatrician. Obsession is a sign of postpartum anxiety.

If your baby is peeing and pooping, gaining weight, and seeming happy, do not obsess about their weight. Because of my struggles with breast-feeding, the use of the nipple shield, and the early weight checks, I began to constantly obsess over whether he was eating enough. Although my lactation consultant and pediatrician told me that he was growing and eating well, I was still obsessed.

I was a lactation nurse, so I thought breastfeeding would come easily to me. I teach a breastfeeding class to new moms! But at this point, all my knowledge and experience didn't matter. That's anxiety! I weighed him at home every week to ensure he was gaining weight. This added more stress to my life. If your doctors tell you your baby is healthy, do not obsessively measure their weight.

My postpartum anxiety was a torturous cycle. The crippling anxiety drove me to want to control every single thing that happened to my son. I tried to control every minute of his day. I wanted to ensure that every single thing he ate, did, and experienced was in a controlled environment because I thought nothing bad would happen to him if I was in charge. Any change in his schedule made me anxious. If he didn't sleep the exact amount of time he was supposed to at nap time, it was devastating. If he didn't eat for longer than 5 to 10 minutes, it was frustrating. Control was my unhealthy anxiety coping mechanism.

TIP: Babies are unpredictable. Find healthy coping mechanisms other than control.

Have you ever looked back at your postpartum journey and not remembered any of it? The parts I remembered most were scary. I felt like a terrible mom all the time. I felt like I couldn't give my son what he needed. Thoughts of my son dying filled my head at least 10 times a day. These images were completely detailed and gory. One was of him lying face down in the pool, blue and drowned. One was of him falling out of my arms onto the concrete floor and busting his head with blood spilling out everywhere. Obviously, suffocating at night without me knowing was another major one as well. I felt like I never slept. I remember thinking if I fell asleep with him on my chest I was going to crush him and he would suffocate. Therefore, sleeping with the baby sleeps did not happen for me. When I was a pediatric emergency nurse, I saw so many babies come into the hospital because of SIDS or suffocation. The thought of this terrified me and placed me on the path of self-destruction.

TIP: Educate yourself and those around you of what is normal "Baby Blues" vs. postpartum anxiety/depression.

The lack of sleep impacted my postpartum anxiety even more. My son only took 20-minute naps for the first three months of his life, and I rarely got a chance to put him down. He wanted to be held constantly. He wanted to sleep in my arms. I would forget to eat most days. I would watch the clock and feel dread around 4:00 each afternoon. I was waiting for my husband's arrival home from work at 5:30 p.m. This was the most challenging time for me because it was the "witching hour," when my son would become uncontrollable and scream. I couldn't bear the crying anymore. I felt like I didn't know how to soothe my own baby. I would beg for my husband to come home early.

In the mornings, before he left for work, I would sit in the rocking chair in my bedroom, tears pouring down my face, sobbing and telling him, "Please don't leave me!" I hated being alone with my son. I am a social person, and I like interaction, so this put me into an even deeper depression and made my anxiety even worse.

The loneliness and guilt continued to intensify my anxiety. When Miles was 7 weeks old, my support system wasn't able to be there for me anymore. My mother left for a sabbatical, and my mother-in-law had to take care of her parents. Prior to that my husband went back to work a week after my son was born. I felt alone, scared, and abandoned. Everyone had gone back to their normal life and left me to navigate my new life without them. I was left at home with this newborn that I did not know anything about or how to take care of. I had self-isolated in fear of a screaming newborn and lack of control of the outside world.

When I got in the car, my son would cry in the car seat constantly. This made me not want to get in the car anymore. I never left the house unless I absolutely had to. For six months, I was isolated at home. I was constantly pumping, constantly breast-feeding, and constantly trying to stick to a schedule. I felt like I was on a hamster wheel and I couldn't get off.

A few years later, I was encouraged by my therapist to talk to my husband and mother about my feelings. I told them both that I had felt abandoned. It wasn't anything they had done wrong. They were amazing and loving to me always, however it was my own lack of mother-confidence that led me to the feeling of abandonment. They were going on with their normal life. I felt left behind. I felt no one else's life had changed as dramatically as mine. Just by talking with them about this loss, helped me heal. I didn't want them to feel guilty, but I also needed to talk about it to heal.

. . .

At three months postpartum, I begin to lose a significant amount of weight. I dropped to 112 pounds. I had not been that weight since high school. I really hadn't noticed it until my father saw me after two months postpartum and said, "You're way too skinny; what is going on?" Everybody kept telling me I looked great for just having a baby. After I realized that most of my clothes were too loose, I attributed it to the fact that I wasn't getting enough to eat during the day. The reason for that was because I wasn't able to put my baby down all day long. I was putting his eating needs first and not paying attention to mine. Day after day, my husband would get home, and I would then realize that I only ate a snack or two all day. It was always something I could just shove in my mouth while rocking and feeding my baby.

TIP: Pay attention to your physical health and body's needs. Ask for help if you're not able to get the nutritious intake you need while breast-feeding your baby. Set up your "nursing station" with water and whatever pre-packaged snacks you can keep close by. Have frozen meals on hand, or ask someone to deliver you food.

I remember one day when I was about 10 weeks postpartum. My friend came to the house to see the baby, and she brought me lunch. I sat down at 2 o'clock and ravished the meal. I remember it tasting so good and being so happy that she took the time to bring me food. It really came to my attention when another friend looked at me one day and said, "That baby is literally sucking the life out of you." Postpartum anxiety and stress can lead to significant weight loss or significant weight gain. Find ways to make meals easy in the beginning.

TIP: Let others help you; you have not failed as a mother in doing this. Find a way to get out of the house and engage yourself in activities with other mothers.

I had so many friends say to me, "I'll come hold the baby for you while you sleep." Many came to visit in the beginning and provided support, food, and love. I will always remember those friends and appreciate what they did for me. When they offered to hold him so I could nap, I would decline. I worried that if he cried, they wouldn't know what to do because I didn't even know what to do. Or they would get anxious and think he wasn't a good baby because he was crying. I kept declining many offers of help out of pure fear and anxiety. What would other people think if I took their help? Like I couldn't take care of one baby all on my own? Like I wasn't a good mother? Those thoughts were also what stopped me from saying yes to help.

I never called out for help from friends for anything – for extra sleep, making a meal, or just helping me go to the store and do basic things. Anytime I went to a playdate, I would have to gain the confidence to just get in the car with a screaming baby. Each trip home resulted in my son screaming, red-faced, and me sobbing. I carried an extra box of tissues each time we went out. I would stop multiple times on the side of the road to try to console him, feed him or rock him. I have found with most of my patients who encounter postpartum, it is because they isolate themselves from their support system. They miss their friends, and family. They miss the social aspect of life they had before. Around 6 months postpartum I was able to see that this support system of other moms was crucial to my healing. I set up a Facebook page called "Mommin Aint Easy", in hopes to create playdates with my other mom friends. We tried to meet on a weekly basis for playdates. This helped tremendously.

TIP: Sometimes it takes something big, an event or occurrence to truly see that you in fact are not doing well mentally, physically or emotionally.

When Miles was seven months old, we took a trip to San Diego for a wedding and to visit family. This trip opened my eyes. The fear of traveling outside my house and the unknown of what might happen on the trip crippled me. Once we arrived, I remember getting in the car and having significant anxiety about him crying. We were close to his nap-time, and I knew the meltdown was coming. I was right, my son screamed the entire way to our destination. I didn't know what to do. I just tried to calm him by constantly rubbing his head, telling him he was going to be alright, and urging my husband to hurry.

Once arriving, I put him down for a nap. I sat on the floor in the dark room as he fell asleep. I sobbed quietly on the floor curled up, holding my knees to my chest. I didn't understand how this happy time in my life could be so hard. I was around all my family and in this beautiful place, but I couldn't enjoy any of it.

The next day, I had to wake my son up early from his nap to get to a wedding. This was hard for me due to the pressure of having to interrupt his nap and his normal schedule. This led to frustration and more anxiety. The traffic was backed up, and we left slightly late due to prolonging his nap as long as I could. Being late to a wedding was horrifying to me as well. I was in a van with my husband, son, brother, and his new girlfriend. The overwhelming anxiety took over, and I became someone that nobody recognized.

My husband had seen my emotions getting worse, but my brother had not seen this side of me *ever* before. I was screaming at my husband. I was hysterical. I lost control of everything at that moment in time. I had a complete panic attack. Looking back, I didn't know that was what it was, but now, I know it was a true panic attack – my first one. I felt like my head was going to explode and the whole world was caving in on me, making it hard to breathe.

We ended up getting to the wedding on time, and everything was fine, but the overwhelming emotions that consumed me at that point exhausted me as well. I wasn't able to have fun at the wedding. Before the reception I snuck into the bathroom to hide and cry. I usually love weddings! I love to dance! But I hated going to that wedding. It had nothing to do with the wedding itself but the lack of control over my son's environment. I didn't want to have fun, and I didn't want to be around my family. I just wanted to go home and be alone. That's the true definition of postpartum – not enjoying things you enjoyed before.

We left the wedding early, and I remember after putting my son to bed, I hopped in the shower. I spent 30 minutes on the shower floor, sobbing and rocking. I didn't know who I was, and I didn't know what to do about it. I was terrified, embarrassed by how I acted, and truly exhausted.

After that trip, my brother and I didn't talk for a few weeks. I felt as though he totally ignored me on the trip. I felt like he wanted nothing to do with my son. I called him to ask him why, and what he told me broke my heart. He said that he didn't want to be around me. He told me I had changed, and he didn't like the person that I was. He told me that I was mean for yelling at my husband, and he had never seen me act that way before. He later told me he was worried about our marriage.

My brother and I had always been really close, and we were always really supportive of each other. We both have been through many ups and downs in our lives. I always expected him to be there for me. When he wasn't, it was a shock. I was devastated by the way he talked to me. The tears filled my eyes, and all I could say was "I'm sorry." He told me he was disappointed at the way I had treated my husband. I took this as he was disappointed in me as a mother, a sister, and a wife. He told me I needed to get help mentally because I wasn't doing well. Although, in hindsight, this is what I needed to hear, at the moment, it was brutal. That night, I searched for a therapist. It took some time after that to forgive him for the hurtful words he spoke that day. But I was at the lowest point I had ever been, and the severity of the pain that came from his words ignited my courage to seek help.

Tip: Step back and take a look at the way you are treating the ones you love most in your life.

Tip: It may be hard to hear what others have to say about your postpartum anxiety or depression, but listen to the ones who love you the most. They can see from the outside.

My postpartum healing journey started after that trip. I found a cognitive behavior therapist to help me with my anxiety and depression after I spoke to my OB/GYN about starting on medication. The medication did have some side effects, but after about four weeks, I felt significantly less anxious. However, the PTSD feelings I had didn't go away. Through therapy, we worked on many areas in my recovery and healing. Some included the feelings of abandonment by my own husband and mother, feeling let down by my brother, and letting go of things I could not control. I call myself a recovering perfectionist. I also did four sessions of hypnotism. I was skeptical at first, but this helped me heal just as much consciously and subconsciously. I'm so thankful for my therapist and recommend to anyone to seek one who they trust.

Tip: Medications may help, but make sure you obtain cognitive behavior therapy as well.

You can't just expect to take medicine and see a therapist a few times. You have to put in the work in order to heal. If you truly want to decrease your risk of postpartum depression and/or anxiety the next time around, put in the work. It took me over a year with my therapist and six months taking medication to overcome my postpartum anxiety and depression. I worked really hard, had lots of homework, did a lot of self-care, and also looked in the mirror every day. I am still working hard to be a better me with all the techniques I learned in therapy..

Tip: If money is not a factor, take as much time off of work as you can.

Years later, when my daughter was born, I had so much help, and it was wonderful. My mother-in-law and my mother would come and stay with me during the weekend, along with our nanny during the week. During the time I was due to deliver, COVID happened. This was terrible for the world and for a lot of people, but for me, it was a blessing because my husband got eight extra weeks at home with us. This gave us time to grow and bond as a family and meant so much to me. It is terrible that women and men do not have the time to be off of work to bond with their children in the beginning. I believe this leads to a lot of postpartum anxiety and depression. The extra support and time at home allows a mother to bond and heal.

Tip: If you're not interested in medication, find other natural treatment options.

With my second child, I decided not to start on medication right away, although many providers recommend it. Because I was so aware of my past and had done the work, I knew I may not need the medication. I had all the tools in my hand and would reach out if I needed them. I did have some postpartum depression more than anxiety with my daughter. I researched and found a local place for my postpartum recovery to perform transcranial magnetic stimulation. I started the process at five months postpartum. It consisted of 36 sessions over about five months. This helped me significantly and was covered by my insurance. After the first few sessions, I instantly felt a difference and knew I chose the right treatment. I sought out a counselor again. The process of treating my postpartum was much shorter than with my son because I started early.

Other natural remedies and coping mechanisms I used included exercise and a healthy, nutritional diet. Supplements I took included ashwagandha, iron, vitamin D, B12 complex, and magnesium. Ask your doctor for a complete blood work panel. My ferritin level was very low, and that can lead to postpartum mental health issues. All I needed to take to improve that was calm iron. Ask your provider to check your thyroid as well.

TIP: Give yourself grace.

I love the mom that I am today. I'm not perfect, and that's okay. I still have a lot to learn and more to work on. I'm accepting the challenge and enjoying each lesson. Today, I am able to truly enjoy moments with my kids and immerse myself in the crazy. This is the feeling I was missing as a first-time mother. I lacked mother-confidence. Anxiety took that away from me. But I will not be sad for those moments lost. I will take what I have learned and progress. I wouldn't be the person I am today if I didn't walk through the dark to find the light again. Because of my experiences, I am able to help hundreds of women like me. I can relate to them and tell them they are not alone, and together, we can make each other stronger.

As I look in the mirror today, I recognize the woman looking back at me. I love her most days. Each day presents a challenge with children. We are always learning and growing as parents. Remember to give yourself grace. Know you are the best parent for your child. They chose you. They love you, imperfections and all.

ABOUT THE AUTHOR

Constance Lewis is now a mother of three beautiful children, thanks to the amazing science behind fertility treatments. Her true passion, other than being a mother, is taking care of other women. Women who have suffered or are suffering the same path as she. She is a Women's Health Nurse Practitioner, Fertility Coach, Pediatric Sleep Coach, and Postpartum Support Coach. She has her own consulting business online and works in a private women's gynecology and obstetrics office. Before that she worked as a nurse in the neonatal ICU for over 10 years. She also served as a nurse educator, manager, childbirth educator, breastfeeding counselor, and community health educator. Her educational journey uniquely coincided with her own personal infertility struggle, a struggle that might have been insurmountable except for the determination that served her well in her career. Her passion for supporting women through her work as an NP, specifically women who struggle with infertility, has never subsided, even after she and her husband have been blessed with their own children. Each personal struggle in her life has pushed her to become educated in each of her specialties so that she may help others. Outside of her family and career, she enjoys CrossFit, traveling, sports, music, and spending time with those she loves.

4

REBIRTH: TRANSCENDING POSTPARTUM DEPRESSION TO DISCOVER PURPOSE

ARIELLE MARTONE

I'm not one for regrets; I don't find them helpful, but one I'm not sure I can shake fully is not having my kids know their Poppy John, my dad. My solace is now that my two babies are here, I truly believe they are exactly who I was waiting for and that the timing was what it needed to be to bring these two special lights into my world. I have to believe this.

I am what you might consider a type "A" person — focused, driven, and determined. I'm someone who might be considered hot, quick-tempered, fiery, or, as I like to phrase it, passionate. When I knew I wanted to attend graduate school, it needed to be a top Ivy League school, and after starting my career, I needed to become a specialist in my field. When I started running, I kept pushing my edge until I eventually ran 50 miles. Once I knew I wanted to be with my husband, nothing was going to deter me. I'm like this in most areas of my life, the exception being my yoga practice, the one space I've been able to set my ego aside.

Motherhood was never front of mind for me. I told myself I had other ambitions, but honestly, I had some reservations. I wasn't sure if I was cut out for it or if I was selfless enough or good enough.

My mother was a stay-at-home mom. She seemed happy enough

while we were younger, but I know she struggled as we left, and I feel like a part of this is because she lost herself in motherhood, at least to a point. Motherhood was her martyrdom. She did a lot for us, trying to give us more than she had as a kid. My sisters and I were far from oblivious of that fact — something my mother made sure of.

I was fearful of losing myself, of giving up everything I worked so hard for. I let my fear, as well as my doubts (and I had many of them) dictate my path, putting family life on hold for maybe longer than I would have otherwise. I dove full into all the other things I felt I *should be* doing, things I knew HOW to do.

> *TIP: It is always best to confront our fears rather than try to hide or outrun them. The truth is we can't outrun our fears; they eventually catch up. As hard as it might be, once we start to confront our fears, they start to have less power over us.*

My husband, Billy, and I were together for years before committing to starting a family. We were both so focused on our schooling and getting our careers started that we decided it would not be the right time for a while. Growing our family was not front of mind, until it was. Once we committed to that journey, starting a family quickly became all-consuming.

Billy and I were finally in a place where we thought it made sense to start a family. The timing seemed "right." We were both stable in our careers, had purchased a home, and I finally felt more ready. My desires for a family finally outweighed my fears that I might be too selfish to be a mother.

Time is a funny thing; we try so hard to control it and make it work for us. The truth is there is never a right or perfect time for anything. You may never feel ready for anything; conversely, you might want to jump right into everything. Neither is wrong. Time seems to unfold as it needs to. This is never more apparent than when going through the process of freezing embryos and having time literally stand still for my future babies.

> *TIP: Easier said than done, but try to avoid regrets. You can work towards this by moving away from shaming yourself around "the right time" and also by trying to stay present. Presence in your life is key to everything. There are so many other moments and events that will occur while you are on this infertility journey, and you deserve to enjoy those events. You deserve to have plenty of happy days mixed in with your struggles. Remember that there is no right or wrong time. Try to let go of your expectations around when you think you "should" be a mother or the spacing between your children's ages if you are trying for multiple children. For me, I have to believe that timing, although it didn't make sense to me at the time, was exactly what it needed to be.*

It was during this time of no longer trying to **not** become pregnant that we lost my dad to cancer. My dad was a wonderful father and an even better Poppy. When I said goodbye to him, I mourned my loss of him and also mourned all the could-have-beens, especially him not getting to know my children.

That year, amid losing my dad, relocating for work, and settling into a new job and a new home, Billy and I got serious about starting a family. Months ensued of checking my body temperature and urinating on ovulation sticks (something I hated with a passion).

Trying to conceive started to make sex feel contrived. Little did I know, this was only the beginning. Month after month, I would get my period. After about six months of no success, which was preceded by over a year of "let's see what happens," we decided to seek additional support through Boston IVF. This was the start of our four-year saga where trying to become a mother was no longer something to be avoided or feared but something I dedicated my life to. Before I knew it, trying to conceive (with a diagnosis of infertility) took over everyday life. Even with the best attempts to "just relax" (and I tried everything to relax — acupuncture, yoga, meditation), I couldn't shake loose the grip it had on me.

I know how to get what I want — just ask my husband. I'm persistent. I research. I plan to do "the right steps." In this nature, I became consumed with the process. I was going to be a "good student." Here's the thing with infertility, though, it doesn't really care if you are a good student, if you are doing all the right things; you are not guaranteed that A.

My first round of blood work came back with extremely elevated prolactin levels. Everything else seemed to be normal, and my husband's work-up came back without issues. I couldn't get pregnant because my body thought I was in early stages postpartum and actively breastfeeding.

The next step was an MRI to rule out a brain tumor. I recall sitting there in my hospital gown, alone, as my husband was unable to get out of work, trying to calm myself down with deep breathing and rational thoughts. I told myself, "Even if it is a tumor, pituitary tumors are usually benign." My hands were sweaty as I laid there listening to the clucks of the machine despite the classical music playing in my ears. The results were negative, thank God.

As relieved as I was to get the news, I was also frustrated. There seemed to be no actual reason preventing me from becoming pregnant. I started on the medicine Cabergoline and was instructed to continue with actively trying, aka timing sex as meticulously as possible. Follow-ups revealed that the medication was working, and my levels were normalized. Still, I had no double lines, only regular periods.

Throughout that first year of starting at Boston IVF, I had regular visits and blood work, constant monitoring, and procedures including polyp removal and a hysterosalpingography. Other than the elevated prolactin and the polyps, both of which were addressed and "fixed," there was no reason my husband and I should have been having the trouble we were. We were given the diagnosis of **unexplained infertility**. This was infuriating! Give me a problem, and I can try to fix it, but with the unknown, the unexplained it seemed harder to cope. Did I ask for this? Did my hesitation and fear play into my difficulty I was having; I couldn't help but blame myself at least a little.

As we were still having no success even with everything "looking good," we moved into IUI trials — three to be exact. This is where I began to feel my world was put on hold. I was frustrated. Did I say that already? It felt like I was already sacrificing myself, and I wasn't even a mother yet. Timing is everything from here on out, and trying to conceive takes over your calendar. My days, weeks, and even months were at the mercy of my blood work and hormone levels. Making plans for anything became daunting. Thoughts began to sound like, "If this round works, great! We can then make plans for that vacation we were thinking of, but if it doesn't, then we will have to wait X weeks and possibly start again on Y date; if the stars align, we might be good to go at Z date. Then comes the two week wait..." It was exhausting on top of the physical exhaustion your body is feeling due to hormonal shifts each cycle.

It is easy to get caught up in the scheduling and have it consume your day to day. I had to do something different; I refused to let this process fully control me. I did my best to squeeze in everything I could between cycles. I planned vacations and attended holidays and events. I finally signed up for yoga teacher training, something I had wanted to do for ages. I made sure to schedule time for myself. I started to see some of my treatment as self-care, specifically my acupuncture days.

TIP: Remember what I discussed previously concerning timing. It is easy to get caught up with it, but do your best to schedule things for yourself. Having something to look forward to other than a potential baby can do wonders for your overall mood and well-being.

For the most part, I was able to make it work. My planner became my best friend, and I was able to work around the blood work, injections, and visits.

Our last IUI trial fell victim to scheduling conflicts. We had my sister-in-law's wedding in Philadelphia. What should have been a fun event and a joy for me to be a part of was overtaken by the stress and, yes, even some anger that our procedure needed to be canceled. We were instructed to continue with my injections and timed intercourse. Needless to say, it was another negative pregnancy test and a blur of a weekend.

After three failed IUIs, it was time to start the IVF process. The egg retrieval process made me feel and look pregnant for several weeks. We were lucky, though; the procedure itself went smoothly, and they got 13 quality eggs that resulted in eight good embryos.

The hours after the procedure were fine — movies and salty snacks (doctor's orders!). However, that ease quickly faded as my body became restless during the five-day wait for the fresh transfer and then the two-week wait after that. During that time, I was not able to work out the way I would have liked. I listened, and I knew the risk of ovarian torsion was real and so not worth it. It doesn't make it any easier, though, when exercise is your go-to mood booster and stress relief.

The transfer failed, and our hearts sank again. Another look at my blood work showed borderline elevated clotting factors. They were at the high end of normal, and worth addressing to rule out possible complications. I started on blood thinners in addition to all the hormone injections for subsequent trials. I also started regular weekly acupuncture, along with the pre- and post-transfer acupuncture our clinic offered.

The second transfer was a success! We had positive HCG levels, and I was pregnant! That joy was short lived as the follow up test did not show HCG levels increasing as they are supposed to. It was termed a chemical pregnancy, as if it didn't really exist. To me, it did. It was real; it was hope and heartbreak all in one.

During this time, I continued to look into what else I could do for a successful outcome. I continued with acupuncture, took herbal supplements in addition to prenatal vitamins, changed my diet, and became a vegetarian for a whole year. I continued running but took a break from running ultras. I meditated more and kept consistent with my yoga practice. I was trying to find more ease, and at the same time, there was frustration that I already had to put my life on hold. I know it sounds crazy, but I enjoyed running 32 and 50 miles, and I know so many people who do and are able to get pregnant on their own. Why couldn't I?

Throughout the IVF process and with each failed transfer, I would try to change or adjust something else. *Finally*, all that adjusting seemed to pay off. At my third transfer, I lay there, feet up in stirrups, watching the procedure on screen, looking for the "sparkle." As we waited a few moments for the team to double check the pipette, once again hopeful for our future, we were informed that they needed to re-do the transfer. What? We apparently had a sticky embryo, and it remained in the pipette. All the thoughts rushed through my head, but our nurse was wonderful and optimistic, and she was right — this one took!

TIP: Always ask your team to double check the pipette! It may seem silly, but no one cares MORE about your procedure's success than you! Advocate for yourself.

This pregnancy progressed well. During this time, I started to regain control over my own life. I exercised regularly, ate well (although transitioned back towards being an omnivore as I was craving burgers). I made a birth plan and prepared for my ideal birth, which was vaginal and unmedicated. I did prenatal yoga, yoga squats all day, perineal massage, and the therapy ball replaced my couch at the end of the night. I did all the right things, including visualizations of how my birth would go. Then, at 41 weeks with low amniotic fluid, I needed to be induced.

So much for being unmedicated! I was so excited to finally be meeting my baby but felt a pang of disappointment for not going into labor on my own. I was also worried, and my thoughts raced. "Why was my fluid so low?" "Have I been leaking fluid and didn't realize?" "How could I miss that?" "Did I put my baby at risk?" "Was I already a bad mother?"

My team was reassuring, and I trusted them. Other than the low amniotic fluid, everything else was looking good. I was at a baby-friendly hospital, and my team knew my plan and was supportive.

TIP: Make sure you are fully comfortable with your medical team and where you plan to deliver. Ask a lot of questions as you are figuring out who your team will be. You want to make sure their values align with yours, that you trust their expertise, and that you feel heard and understood when you are with them.

After about 10 hours of close, excruciating contractions from the Pitocin, I caved. I needed to either eat or sleep or preferably both. My husband would sneak me pretzels and Gatorade, but that wasn't cutting it. I ended up requesting an epidural, which allowed for some rest. After another 10 hours of labor and three hours of active pushing, I needed an emergency cesarean. I felt like a failure.

I was awake for the delivery of my son, but soon after, I was placed under general anesthesia due to convulsions and significant blood loss. Prior to being put under, I felt gutted, literally and figuratively. I wanted my son on my chest. I wanted skin to skin. I ached to hold my baby, whom I waited so very long for. This was not how my birth story was supposed to go! Why was my body failing me again?

And it continued to fail me. Breastfeeding was important to me, to my son. Our breastfeeding journey was off to a very slow start. I needed to use a nipple shield to have him latch initially. I thought it would be temporary, but it lasted three months. I was so hard on myself. Why was everything that I thought was supposed to come easily and naturally not working for me? Self-doubt crept back in; maybe I wasn't supposed to be a mother after all.

> *TIP: Breastfeeding is a skill, and like any skill, it takes learning and practice. It rarely, if ever, comes "easily" or "naturally" to first-time mothers. Both you and your baby are brand new at this, so give yourself a lot of grace as you are learning, and seek support. Most hospitals in the U.S. have lactation support, so request it early and **often**. If you plan to breastfeed, talk to your physician prior to delivery to set you up with support early on. I found that KellyMom.com and La Leche were both very good free resources.*

I did my best for three months to cope with these feelings, alternating between pushing them down and wallowing in them. What I never *actually* did was confront and address them. At the time, I didn't realize that I needed to. I assumed this was normal, just the "baby blues," and it may have been, but the truth is, even if it was just the baby blues, I should have addressed it. As breastfeeding took off, I began to feel better and slowly gained confidence in my abilities as a mother. But was I comfortable enough to do it again? And was I ready to go through it all again? I wasn't sure.

Back when my husband and I sat down to discuss starting a family we always talked about having more than one. Of course, the reality of needing to do IVF can make starting and then expanding a family daunting. This weighed heavily on me from the beginning. I knew how long and difficult it was to have my first, and I wanted to try sooner than later, but I felt frozen in self-doubt. As I settled in, I became comfortable enough with motherhood that I felt ready to try again.

You hear stories of people who need to do IVF for their first and then, poof, as if by magic, get pregnant on their own. We actually know two of those lucky couples. That was not our story (though it was not for lack of trying). To grow our family, we needed to once again seek medical support through IVF. Three additional embryos, one of which was lost in the defrost phase, and two transfers later, we were blessed with another pregnancy — this time as a geriatric pregnant patient.

Such as life sometimes goes for us old ladies, this pregnancy wasn't as smooth. Due to a low-lying placenta and scarring from my cesarean, there were talks of needing another c-section with the possibility of a hysterectomy. Going through IVF, I am fully aware of the fact that my husband and I alone do not dictate the size of our family, and I went into this pregnancy knowing full well that this might be and likely was my last pregnancy. But hysterectomy? There was something heart wrenching about any possibility of having more children being removed completely and permanently. Fortunately, with time and imaging, my placenta shifted and was no longer at risk of attaching to my scarring. Against the odds of low-lying placenta and a baby who never seemed to want to be head down, I was able to have a successful VBAC, (vaginal birth after cesarean).

Everything seemed to go "right" this time around. I had a vaginal birth, did skin to skin right away, and was able to get my baby girl to latch immediately. I was elated and overcome with joy of the process and for my daughter and son. If everything went right this time, why did I feel so down? I mean, I asked for this; I *REALLY ASKED* for this.

The thoughts came flooding back at an unstoppable rate — not being good enough, not being meant for this, not being what my babies needed. Was I happy? Sort of. I loved my babies, and I bonded with both easily, and fiercely; yet, I felt off. I was lost, I missed my old life, I didn't know how to identify myself outside of my professional labels, and I was exhausted and depleted. I felt angry despite all the good in my life, and my fuse was short. My patience for my son's tantrums was at an all-time low, and my patience for my husband was non-existent. Everything he did or did not do seemed wrong and frustrated me.

> *TIP: If you experience any of the above, first, know that you are not alone; it is very common. It is normal to mourn the old version of yourself. Allow yourself space and time to do that*

without guilt. Two things can be true — you can feel grateful for being a mother, and you can miss your more carefree days. Feeling one emotion does not negate the other. I found journaling to be very helpful to process my mixed emotions as well as learning to lean into the hard rather than turning away from it, reframing what I needed to, and also allowing myself time to heal and recover postpartum. There is often a feeling of needing to "bounce back" or rush through this postpartum period. It doesn't allow for processing of our new roles, new bodies, and adjustments to our new relationship. This is exactly why I shifted careers and went into postpartum coaching — to provide new moms with the support they deserve. If you are struggling with adjusting postpartum, know that it is common, often normal, and you absolutely can get support, whether from myself or another coach, doula, or healthcare provider.

I wanted to stay home with my kids; that was my choice from the beginning. Plus, it was way too early to even consider going back to work. Still, I became resentful of my husband for being out of the house, able to escape, able to feel like himself. That was the biggest part when I boil it all down — not the being at work per se but just not feeling like myself and not having the words to fully describe it or a way in which to cope.

Aside from the emotional turmoil, I physically wasn't feeling like myself either. I am well aware of the physical changes, the healing and recovery that needs to happen to feel like myself again. The reshifting of our organs, the healing vaginal tissue, the time to re-engage abdominals, the weeks for my pelvis to begin to narrow. Knowing and implementing can be two very different things.

After the initial awkwardness of my postpartum body, the adjustments that occur, and the discomfort of the healing stitches, I still didn't feel like myself. After being cleared at eight weeks, my husband and I attempted intercourse. I had intense vaginal discomfort that halted any enjoyment. I had some serious work to do to regain pleasure — in all areas of my life.

I also wanted to get back to running but knew that step one was eliminating vaginal pain first. I knew that pain is common after childbirth but that it is not normal. I also knew there are ways to heal and move past it. What I didn't know nor expect was the frustration I would feel having to do the work, take the time I needed, and push off intimacy even longer.

It may seem contradictory to long for a return to intimacy with my husband when everything he did aggravated me (and let me be clear, he really wasn't doing anything wrong.) I felt like maybe if we were able to resume a more intimate relationship, it would help me not be so angry with him, that he would feel more like my partner again and less like a roommate. Also, sex is important to me; it helps me connect with my husband, I enjoy it (or used to anyway), and it's just one of the ways I feel like me, something that was taken from me in seemingly every aspect of my life.

> *TIP: While it is very common to have a decreased sex drive immediately postpartum, it is not normal for it to be drastically decreased from your baseline for several months after baby. Your sex drive (while it can vary from day to day) is a good indicator of your overall wellness. Any sudden, drastic change in it is a sign that you need to dig a little deeper to see what is going on. Common reasons for drop in sex drive postpartum are fatigue, feeling touched out, vaginal dryness, pelvic or vaginal pain, traumatic birth, symptoms of depression or anxiety, resentment for your partner ... the list can go on, but all of this can be addressed and dealt with. A low libido is not another thing to chalk up to "mom life," and addressing it can be a big piece in feeling like yourself again.*

I was mad at myself for being "preoccupied" with all of these thoughts and feelings. This led to so much guilt, knowing I was one of the lucky ones. I had two babies through IVF when so many hopeful mamas don't reach that goal. The intense guilt shifted to shame, which just perpetuated the spiral of depression and rage.

TIP: Guilt is just information, and when we take it in and look at why we might be feeling guilty without tacking on biases or expectations, we can see where some of our values are, see what changes could be made, and move forward and grow. However, when we wallow in guilt and feel guilty for the guilt, it can quickly spiral into shame, and not much productive comes of that. Note that you are entitled to your feelings, regardless of what other people may or may not be struggling with. Your infertility successes do not limit other people's chances at success, and your struggles do not negate the struggles of others. When you lean into that, you can start giving yourself permission for your own experiences and, with that, some grace.

Rage/anger is also just information and does not need to be demonized postpartum — or any time, really. We should always check in with ourselves as to why we are feeling this way. What are we angry about, and what is triggering us into bouts of rage? Knowing the causes can lead us to understand more clearly our values, what we are passionate about, and where we might need help. Feeling rage or anger is never a problem, but how we deal with it might need to be addressed.

On top of all the emotional upheaval, I constantly felt like I was failing either my son or my daughter and neither was getting what I felt they deserved. I felt sure that someone else could do this mothering better for them. I felt like I was failing myself and my husband. Clearly, he, too, deserved better. I fantasized about running away, and I was shocked by my desire to escape.

Admitting these things was the first step towards overcoming it. With Billy's encouragement, I reluctantly started speaking with a therapist. It was difficult for me to admit that I had a "problem" or that something was "wrong" with me. It felt shameful admitting I was struggling with becoming a mother, something I strived for so long to achieve. I started to take control of my physical recovery and dove fully into self-development books, podcasts, and coaching. I committed to being that *good student* again.

This was all helpful to a point, but I did not fully start to piece myself back together until I began to rely more heavily on my yoga background and take in information with the intent to learn and grow rather than perfect and conquer. My yoga practice was vital for that shift.

I started to resume my breath work and physical practice. I began to really bridge my mind-body connection and live in the philosophies of the power of staying present in the current situation and also in my body. I leaned back into my yoga teacher training and the Rasas (The Yoga of Nine Emotions), which emphasizes that there is good and bad or two sides to all emotions. This gave me permission to be myself, to acknowledge what I was feeling, and to stop labeling myself as bad or flawed.

For so long during the infertility and IVF process, our bodies and our lives feel as though they are not ours. They are put on hold, and it can be really difficult to reclaim them, especially early in postpartum when we, at times, already feel like we are still not ourselves. However, it is essential that we do so. At no fault of our own, women who go through IVF are at a higher risk of postpartum mood disorders. I truly believe that we owe it to ourselves and our families to commit to the work of allowing our hearts, minds, and bodies to mend. It takes time and some effort, but it is so worth it.

I have since come to terms with myself and the mother I am becoming. I feel like myself — not exactly myself pre-babies but my true honest self. I am a bit different now, but I no longer mourn for the old version of me. I fully accept this new more open version. My body also feels like mine again, even at 20 months postpartum as I am still breastfeeding my daughter and have not returned to my pre-baby size. I feel strong and connected. I fully resolved my vaginal pain within four months. I have been able to complete a difficult trail half marathon without pain and with a personal record. I am able to hold challenging yoga poses for long periods of time and have been pushing into heavier lifting at the gym.

My relationship with my husband is stronger than it has been. We have worked really hard on honest and productive communication. He was willing to learn and grow alongside me. Since feeling more confident in my body and having addressed the vaginal pain, I feel our relationship isn't only more connected but more passionate as well.

I now finally feel confident in my ability to parent and trust my maternal instincts. Do I have the occasional moments of doubt or mom guilt? Absolutely, but those moments are short lived, and I now have the confidence that I will figure it out and that I can always repair and make a different choice as needed. By returning to my body, I am able to address those negative thoughts that sprinkle in from time to time and confront the doubt in a productive manner.

There is a great peace that comes from acceptance of who one is and understanding that there is always learning and growth but no need to strive for unrealistic perfection. Through this whole messy journey of postpartum after IVF, confronting the challenges and learning to give myself grace, and figuring out a way to heal and rebuild, I can say with a full heart that it was so worth it. This journey has provided so much insight and growth. It has forged me into a better partner, a more compassionate version of myself, and — dare I say it? — even a good enough mother.

ABOUT THE AUTHOR

Arielle Martone is a doctor of physical therapy, neuro-clinical specialist, certified yoga teacher, and certified pre- and postnatal coach turned postpartum wellness coach after overcoming her own postpartum depression and pelvic pain. Her postpartum journey highlighted the importance of allowing time for healing the emotional and physical and really reconnecting mind and body, which is why she created The Postpartum Revolution™. Arielle now helps new moms feel amazing in their bodies and confident in who they are becoming so they can stop second guessing themselves and start enjoying motherhood.

5

HOW I THREW AWAY MY CRUTCHES

MACKENZIE FRASER

Hi. My name is Mackenzie*, (or at least that's the name you will know me by as you read my story) and I am a recovering alcoholic.

You might hate me after reading my story. I hated myself for a very long time. I'm writing it in the hope that many people might benefit from it – whether directly or indirectly.

I was never the stereotypical image of an alcoholic. I did not drink in the mornings or during working hours. I did not even drink daily – until much later. However, when I did drink, it seemed that I did not have an "off" switch. This did not happen every time I drank, and therefore, I thought I had it under control for many years. I have learned since my healing journey started six years ago that alcoholism is a progressive illness. For some, it progresses faster than for others.

I suspected that I had an unhealthy relationship with alcohol a long time before I would admit the real extent of the problem to myself. A lot of time and alcohol-related trauma had to pass for me to finally admit my problem to my long-suffering husband and others. I had a loving husband and family, a fulfilling job, a home, two dogs, wonderful friends, and a daughter who we had longed for, prayed for, struggled for, and begged for. By God's grace, I still have all those things. But I came very close to losing it all.

How did it come to this? What happened to me? According to renowned addiction expert, Dr. Gabor Maté, "All addicts have experienced trauma, but not everyone who has experienced trauma will become addicts." I could write a book about my trauma and our journey to parenthood, and I wish I could go into more detail in this chapter. Perhaps I feel that providing those details would somehow justify my alcoholism.

If I had to pinpoint when the disease started, I would say it was in my late twenties. I had a miscarriage of a precious pregnancy conceived after more than a year of trying to get pregnant. During the year that followed, I discovered how helpful alcohol was at numbing my emotions. I have experienced bouts of depression and anxiety in the past. However, I plunged into a deep depression after losing our little baby. At that time, one could have described me as a binge drinker. I would often have quite a few too many glasses of wine during an evening out.

> *Tip: Allow yourself time to grieve a pregnancy loss. Seek counseling or at least a supportive, understanding person to speak to. Ignoring the emotions or blaming yourself delays healing. Do not diminish what you are going through.*

A year or so later, we decided to try to conceive again, but no matter how we tried or the advice we followed, nothing seemed to work. Unfortunately, it took us a long time to seek the necessary help. At age

32, we finally consulted with a fertility specialist. After the fertility clinic ran the full battery of tests on both my husband and me, we got the awful diagnosis of premature ovarian failure (POF). I was in perimenopause and had the "ovaries of a 50-year-old."

This diagnosis was a massive shock for us. We had expected that we might need some medical intervention but never imagined we would get news like this. The fertility specialist recommended that we try IVF with donor eggs (DE). We were devastated. I felt like I was defective, barren. I broke down outside our car in the underground parking garage of the fertility clinic, and my husband cried with me. We stood there holding each other for a long time before we drove home feeling numb. I have often wondered how much heartache and tears those parking garage walls at the fertility clinic have seen. It became the norm for me to regularly use alcohol to numb my emotions with each failed cycle, with each piece of bad news, and in general to quell my fear and anxiety.

Tip: Take time to grieve the loss of a genetic link to your future child or the fact that you need fertility treatment or whatever help you choose to conceive if you feel that you need to.

Infertility shook my faith. I started doubting that God cares about me. Why would He allow this? Why does it seem so easy for people who do not care about their children to conceive? For rapists to further torture their victims by impregnating them. Why does God allow abusers to have children and then allow those children to suffer? If He is omnipotent, does He not decide what happens to us? If He already knows our story, is He not controlling it? I had so many questions. And the **questioning and doubt** filled me with intense feelings of guilt. In turn, the guilt caused me to feel ashamed. I felt as though I didn't deserve to have children. I was in a downward spiral of despair, hopelessness, and self-loathing.

. . .

Throughout my life, I battled poor self-esteem, took everything personally, and lacked confidence. Much later, through therapy, I learned that many of my personality traits can be attributed to childhood trauma. After my POF diagnosis, I started hating myself and my body. I did not take care of myself physically or mentally. I often flew into a rage when I had been drinking, and I started drinking alone at home. Wine became my biggest comfort. I always thought of myself as a sophisticated drinker, but I was gulping down the wine like I couldn't get enough. I looked forward to that feeling of oblivion, forgetting, not feeling.

My alcohol consumption became a very sore point between my husband and me. He felt quite helpless about this problem or how to help me. His opinion was that I should be able to control my drinking with willpower and that it was a choice for me to behave this way. No one else expressed any concern about my drinking habit until after I had stopped. I suspect they probably had an opinion about it at the time, but for whatever reason, they didn't feel comfortable talking to me about it or perhaps didn't quite realize the extent of the problem. My husband clung to the hope that this problem with alcohol would be resolved once we were successful at achieving our dream of becoming parents.

I recently read an article that referred to an addiction to alcohol as "alcohol use disorder (AUD)," which, in my mind, has a less negative label than "alcoholic." Alcohol use disorder (also known as alcoholism) is a pattern of alcohol use that involves the inability to control your drinking, being preoccupied with alcohol, or continuing to use alcohol to the detriment of your health, safety, and quality of life and the safety of others.

Tip: If you suspect you or someone you love has a problem with alcohol consumption or any other addiction, there are many avenues of help. Doctors, psychologists, or religious institutions will be able to put you in touch with professionals or organizations that may be of assistance.

Eventually, we decided to move on to the next step – choosing a donor. Choosing was just the first step of the next step, and unfortunately, our journey to parenthood was not a short one. We ended up doing seven DE IVF cycles over four years, using six different donors, before our beautiful daughter was finally born. Those years were filled with more disappointment and heartache than anyone should have to endure. There were always more questions, more trauma, more rage, and more wine. With each failed cycle, I would buy myself a bottle of fancy French champagne and drink it by myself on the patio through my tears. I told myself that champagne should not be just for celebrating.

I was a very angry person. When I got drunk, I raged — at the unfairness of it all, at all the ignorant things people would say to me, at the platitudes, at the numerous times I was asked how far along my pregnancy was when my belly was bloated because of medication. During one of my rages, I was hitting myself in the stomach, screaming at my horrible, broken body for not being able to give me what I wanted. Do I sound like a petulant child? In another instance, I was slapping myself in the face. I hated myself so much. My gentle giant of a husband had to pin me down with his arm across my chest to stop me from hurting myself. My chest was painful for days afterward because of the strength with which he had to hold me down. Do I sound insane? I think I might have been at that point.

The more I drank, the more depressed I became. And the more depressed I became, the more I drank, fueling my anger and disgust for myself. In hindsight, I have often wondered whether we went through so many failed cycles due to my alcohol consumption. But that does not explain why the last cycle was successful. I am still amazed at how the depression lifted shortly after I stopped consuming alcohol.

> *Tip: Whatever your diagnosis, while going through the infertility journey, consider seeking counseling from a psychologist especially one with a background in treating patients with fertility issues. I found it invaluable to have a safe space in which to talk with someone not emotionally involved in the journey. Cultivate healthy coping mechanisms and ways to relieve your stress, rather than trying to numb your emotions.*

In due course, our fertility specialist, whom we respected and trusted implicitly, recommended that I undergo regression therapy through hypnosis with Dr. O., a clinical psychologist who specialized in the field.. We were very surprised at this very "unscientific" suggestion, but we were desperate enough to try anything. He suspected there might be an underlying problem preventing me from conceiving.

I started that very traumatic journey thinking that a blockage might exist in some deep part of my subconscious because, perhaps deep down, I was afraid to become a mother or didn't feel I deserved to be one. Dr. O. and I did deal with that subject during our sessions initially. However, he had a suspicion that there was more to this thought pattern.

During one of the sessions, he asked me to look at my womb to see what it looked like. What I described was an ugly pool of black, bubbling sludge. It looked like it had been poisoned. What could have caused it to look like this? Through many hellish sessions, I saw images that I will never forget for as long as I live. My subconscious revealed to me that I was sexually abused on multiple occasions by my mother's brother-in-law when I was a little girl. In one of my memories, I heard a sound that I can describe as my soul screaming. I had suppressed these memories my whole life. This is a self-preservation mechanism subconsciously employed by many who experience trauma.

I recently realized that it was at the time of these revelations that I started drinking to die, not only to numb my emotions. This was the source, the traumatic event that led to my addiction. And this was why my womb looked like it had been poisoned. At this point, I was convinced that God did not care about me. Why would God let this happen to a child?

With Dr. O.'s guidance, I spent a few sessions after that under hypnosis, cleaning up the mess that had been left, until finally, I felt sane enough to try another cycle. My regression therapy process took about nine months. Our next cycle – the only cycle with frozen embryos – failed.

The uncle, my abuser, died of prostate cancer the following December. We finally got our positive pregnancy results two months later after our seventh DE IVF. The monster who abused me was dead, and the little girl was safe and free at last.

I had an easy, blissful pregnancy. I felt like our nightmare was over, and we could move forward as a family at last. I did not drink a drop of alcohol during my pregnancy. I was nervous about becoming a mom, as first-time mothers often are, but very excited.

I so desperately wanted something about this journey to motherhood to be "normal." I wanted to give birth vaginally with as little intervention as possible, and I wanted to breastfeed for as long as possible. Unfortunately, it didn't work out like that. Our daughter was born by non-elective cesarean about 24 hours after I was induced. I struggled to breastfeed her from the outset. She struggled to latch, and I struggled with milk supply. But she was the cutest little baby, and she made it all worthwhile. She seemed happy to be alive from the start, and we were just so delighted to have her with us at last.

I've never felt like she is not my daughter. It feels like we were always meant to be together. While I do think of our egg donor occasionally, the fact that we had help from an egg donor is often far from my mind. It took me a long time to admit to someone that I frequently felt disconnected from my daughter, and I felt very guilty about this. I often felt inadequate as a mother and wished motherhood was easier. I learned years later in therapy that this disconnected feeling was a symptom of postnatal depression and PTSD.

Our joy was quickly stolen, and once again, we were living a nightmare when our beautiful baby girl was diagnosed with a rare congenital heart defect at five weeks old. The doctors told us she would eventually require surgery. We were distraught at this news. After all that we had already gone through, we couldn't believe we'd have to face this as well. In the following six weeks, she ended up in NICU twice more with pneumonia, and the doctors told us that she would continue to become ill until her heart defect was corrected. We felt so helpless.

They wanted to wait until she was 6 months old or weighed 5kg before operating, but her frequent NICU stays led to her undergoing open-heart surgery at eleven weeks old, weighing only 3.5 kg. She was so tiny. I have never been as terrified as I was on the day of her heart operation. I tried my very best to keep it together, even though I wanted to curl up in a corner and cry. I had to be strong for our daughter.

While she was in the ICU before and after her surgery, we could only visit her for a total of 45 minutes per day. People would ask me how I remained so strong, and I would reply, "What choice do I have?"

The reality was that I was coping by drinking. Alcohol was the crutch I used to get through every day. My drinking problem had followed me from our infertility journey into motherhood.

> *Tip: If you are going through very stressful or traumatic experiences, allow yourself the time to let out your emotions. Cry, scream, or express your fear in a safe space. Suppressing or numbing your emotions could make the trauma worse. Find a safe person to speak to, and cultivate healthy coping mechanisms instead of finding crutches to help you get through each day.*

Because we struggled with breastfeeding, we supplemented with formula. By the time our daughter had heart surgery, I had stopped trying to breastfeed or pump milk for her and permanently switched to formula. I didn't find out until years later that many babies who have heart conditions struggle with breastfeeding. At the time, I thought it was just another way I had failed as a woman and mother.

The heart surgery was a success! Physically, our daughter was on the road to recovery. However, she experienced some repercussions due to the surgery and the fact that she had spent half of her first 11 weeks of life in ICU on her back without the stimulation and parental bonding that babies usually have during that time. There were a lot of challenges in the first few years of her life in terms of her development, and there still are years later. She has anxiety, sensory issues, and some developmental delays, but we are working on those challenges, and she is making wonderful progress. She is a feisty, confident, adorable little chatterbox now. For the first two years, we struggled to feed her. Due to her sensory issues, she would only eat a very small variety of soft foods. Again, I felt like I was failing as a mother. I couldn't give birth without medical intervention, couldn't breastfeed her, and now, I could hardly feed her. Parenthood was a lot more challenging than I had anticipated. It took us quite a while to find a great team of professionals that could help her start overcoming her challenges.

During all of this, it became clearer to me every day that my drinking was a real problem. I was drinking daily and alone, often finishing a bottle of wine in one evening. I tried to control my drinking on my own by employing a lot of strategies many alcoholics try – drinking only on weekends, switching to other alcoholic beverages, or drinking water in between each drink. I would buy only one bottle of wine at a time because I knew that if there was another bottle at home, I would open it that same evening. None of these strategies worked.

Have no doubt that I have never loved anyone as much as I love my daughter. I love her so much that it makes my heart ache. And yet, even that love could not seem to win against the insanity of alcoholism. I put our much-loved and longed-for daughter's life at risk multiple times by driving under the influence with her in the car. I often had blackouts and would not remember anything from the previous evening.

Eventually, my husband had enough, and I realized at last that I could not continue the way I had been. I was severely depressed and often had suicidal thoughts. Sometimes, while in the shower, I would have visions of my blood running down the drain with the water. Once I dreamed I was dead, and I was so happy and relieved, but as soon as I woke, I burst into tears of disappointment.

Soon after my daughter's second birthday, I joined a twelve-step program and have now been sober and in therapy for six years. I found a psychologist who is perfect for me, with whom I have been having weekly sessions helping me heal from my childhood traumas, the nightmare infertility journey, and the events that occurred after the birth of our daughter. She referred me to a psychiatrist, whom I consult regularly to ensure I am on the correct medication. I have been diagnosed with c-PTSD, depression, and generalized anxiety disorder. My psychologist informed me that she is convinced I had postnatal depression in the two years after our daughter's birth. It's a pity that I wasn't seeing a therapist at that time, and it had gone unnoticed.

Tip: Perhaps, if I didn't try so hard to pretend I was okay and was open and honest with those who cared about me about how I really felt, they would have realized sooner that I needed help. If someone had sat me down and convinced me to talk about my real feelings or noticed that I needed help and convinced me to seek that help, perhaps some of the trauma my husband, family, and I went through could have been avoided.

Today, I am often surprised by the person I have become. I work hard at my sobriety and mental health. I am more confident, and my self-esteem has improved considerably. This is very far removed from the image I had of myself six years ago. I am working on forgiving myself for the mistakes I made and am extremely grateful that those mistakes did not end in tragedy. I don't try to forget the mistakes but use them to remind me of how far I've come and where I never want to go back to. In recovery and with my therapist, I am learning the skills to cope with life in a healthy way that I never had before.

I found God again in recovery. I still have a ways to go, but at least I am on speaking terms with Him. Recently, while listening to the hymn "Amazing Grace," it suddenly dawned on me that, for the first time in my life, I understand what "grace" in the song means. I also realized and believe that God had been there all along. He didn't abandon me, but I started ignoring Him.

I can say without a doubt that my infertility journey broke me, and

I have spent the past few years putting myself back together – for myself and our daughter.

There is so much I have learned in recent years that I wish I had known 20 years ago. I have learned valuable skills for dealing with trauma and the general stress of life, *that gratitude is not a cure for depression*, and how dangerous the "mommy wine club" narrative is. I highly recommend therapy to help you heal from any past traumatic events that might be keeping you stuck. It has saved my life.

I live my life now with this song on repeat in my head, and I'm okay with that.

Amazing Grace
    Amazing grace, how sweet the sound
    That saved a wretch like me
    I once was lost, but now I'm found
    Was blind, but now I see
    'Twas grace that taught my heart to fear
    And grace my fears relieved
    How precious did that grace appear
    The hour I first believed
    Through many dangers, toils, and snares
    I have already come
    This grace that brought me safe thus far
    And grace will lead me home
    When we've been here ten thousand years
    Bright, shining as the sun
    We've no less days to sing God's praise
    Than when we first begun
    Amazing grace, how sweet the sound
    That saved a wretch like me
    I once was lost, but now I'm found
    Was blind, but now I see

ABOUT THE AUTHOR

Mackenzie*, an IT professional, passionately endeavors to dismantle the stigma surrounding infertility and shares her experience, strength, and hope with the still-suffering alcoholic. She'd love to shout from the rooftops about her newfound freedom and happiness in recovery, but she chose to use a pseudonym to protect her daughter's privacy.

"God, grant me the serenity to accept the things I cannot change, the courage to change the things I can, and the wisdom to know the difference. Amen."

* Name changed to protect the innocent

ACKNOWLEDGEMENT

In the creation of this book, 'Infertility Success to Postpartum Mess', there are many individuals whose ceaseless support and dedication have been instrumental. Each one holds a special place in my heart and has left an indelible mark on this journey.

First, my deepest gratitude goes to my husband, Roy, a rock in turbulent seas. His unwavering support and love have been my sanctuary, his belief in me, my guiding light. In those moments when doubt crept in, it was his reassuring voice that spurred me on.

My children, Kingston, Bronson, Preston, and Holden, are the very essence of my inspiration and I thank God for them every day. Their laughter is my melody, their triumphs my own. To them, I owe a debt of gratitude for constantly reminding me of the beauty of motherhood, even amidst its trials.

A profound note of thanks goes out to Melissa Denelsbeck, my editor.

To the brave authors who joined us on this project, your courage and vulnerability in sharing your stories have woven a rich tapestry of experiences. To retrace your steps of early motherhood and endure the pain of those reminders is commendable. While you may not directly witness the impact of your assistance on our readers, rest assured that your contribution will undoubtedly help many navigate their way to brighter horizons.

And finally, to YOU, my dear reader. This book is not just our stories, but it is also a testament of our shared experiences. I thank you for embarking on this journey with us. We are rooting for you and praying for your victory.

BONUS CHAPTER FROM INFERTILITY SUCCESS, STORIES OF HELP AND HOPE FOR YOUR JOURNEY
SEVEN DIAGNOSES AND SEVEN YEARS TO FOUR SONS

ERICA HOKE

If ever there was a woman that was least likely to conceive, it was me. I was over age 35 when I was diagnosed with stage four endometriosis, uterine fibroids, PCOS, thyroid disease, low ferritin, low ovarian reserve, and factor 5 Leiden. With seven contributing infertility diagnoses, I was still considered to have "unexplained infertility." In the back of my mind, IVF was a choice of last resort, or at least it was a choice... until it wasn't.

My husband and I sat in the reproductive endocrinologist office. "You're 35, and you're already hyper-ovulating. Your body is already doing the job that medicine we give you would do. The ultrasound and bloodwork show you have very few eggs left."

"I'm sorry," he said. "You have a better chance of hitting the lottery than getting pregnant." The only option the REI could offer us was IUI, which carried a less than five percent chance of success. Those odds weren't good enough for us, especially since, at that point, we knew my husband's swimmers were "Olympic" level. That's when I started researching anything and everything that affects fertility and then implementing these changes.

TIP: If you're given a poor prognosis with few choices, get another opinion.

That "no" to IVF treatment from our REI wasn't the beginning of our journey. We had been traveling a path to find answers and heal my body from my many reproductive diagnoses for several years. But to understand the full picture, you have to know that my problems started a few years after my first period.

The first memory of the intensity of my periods increasing was Thanksgiving. I rushed from the table to throw up and spent the day in bed. At sixteen, just three years after starting my period, this was "normal" for the first day of my cycle.

The gynecologist offered a prescription for an NSAID and the platitude that the pain was "normal."

TIP: Extreme period pain that includes vomiting, an inability to stand upright, or causes you to miss school or work is not normal and requires additional investigation to determine the medical root cause.

Years later, I was able to see the pattern of what I believed caused the disease that took doctors 15 years to diagnose.

I met my husband one day on a sales call for my job. We were both divorced with no children. When we met, we were both in our early to mid-30s. As our relationship progressed and we spent more time together, he was able to see first-hand what I dealt with on a monthly basis.

Over the 15+ years of having my period, I dealt with the pain mostly by being on hormonal birth control. Convinced this was causing a lot of other symptoms, I decided to stop using it. I was concerned about the long-term effects on my fertility and determined to get my body in the best possible health to carry a baby.

Within months of stopping the pill, my pain had increased to an excruciating level. I was working in outside sales, and my flow was nearly impossible to manage. During a networking lunch, I met a traditional Chinese medicine doctor who practiced acupuncture and would change the course of my life. She assured me that she could help me. It seemed like as soon as I found help, my body went on attack. More than once, my then-boyfriend had to deliver me to her office for treatment while I was sobbing and unable to stand.

In addition to acupuncture, my new gynecologist, although amazing, was ethically bound to only be able to tell me my symptoms *could be* endometriosis or uterine fibroids. Diagnosis meant surgery. Eventually, unable to get relief, I sought out a surgeon who specializes in endometriosis. I was terrified the surgery would cause scarring in my uterus that would prevent me from getting pregnant.

*TIP: If your doctor suspects endometriosis or uterine fibroids, **don't delay** confirming the diagnosis with surgery. DO find a surgeon that will diagnose AND perform the surgical excision at the same surgery.*

We discussed what would happen if she found endometriosis. She let me know that she was one of the few surgeons who would perform the laparoscopic surgery *and* perform the excision surgery. After lots of talking it over and consideration, I decided to have the surgery.

When I woke up from the surgery, the surgeon said she removed *a lot* of endometrioses, stage 4 endometriosis, to be exact. It was the diagnosis I had been waiting 15 years for. It was both inside and outside of my uterus, attached to my ovaries, bladder, and bowels. She was able to see I also had PCOS.

She felt confident that, because of her aggressive surgery, most, if not all, of my problems would be over. She was wrong. While grateful for her skill as a surgeon, the next few months would be some of the most trying of my journey up until that point.

TIP: Before any surgical procedure, any doctor should complete a basic blood panel to confirm your overall health.

Bleeding was to be expected for a few weeks following the surgery, but when a month went by, and my bleeding hadn't stopped, I contacted the surgeon. She sent me home with no suggestions and a "wait and see" attitude. The pain was gone, but for the next 90+ days, I had period-like flow. Little did I know, I was literally bleeding to death.

TIP: If any doctor tells you they can't help you with a problem that seems concerning to you or is disruptive to your life, get a second opinion or keep doing your own research until you find an answer.

I was back to work full time, but I was exhausted. I went to work and came home and headed straight for the couch. Around this time, I drove out of town for work. When I got to the event, I had so much pain in my leg that I couldn't walk. Something was wrong.

A few days later, a red, belt strap looking welt appeared on my leg. I went to see my doctor. After some discussion and hesitation, he decided to send me to the hospital for the ultrasound I didn't receive days earlier when I visited the ER. The ultrasound was inconclusive, and I was admitted to the hospital.

I was so afraid and freaked out. At 33, I was being admitted to the hospital for the first time. The doctor ordered blood work and blood thinners "just in case" I had a blood clot in my leg. A nurse came in to get my blood thinners started, and I was making small talk with her when a tiny voice in my head sounded an alarm.

TIP: If you have an intuition about something or feel something is off, trust your instinct. Always confirm and ask to see any medication being given to you in the hospital.

I looked over at the tray **full** of small vials she was steadily pushing into my IV. I asked, *"Are you going to give me all of that?"* It was a question that saved my life. She looked at me and told me that she would be right back. I never saw her again during my 10-day hospital stay. Instead, a male nurse bustled into the room with an IV pole with a bag of vitamin K hung on it, the antidote to blood thinners.

I had been overdosed by a whole decimal point. Had I not noticed, my organs and brain would have liquefied before the antidote could have been administered.

The lab results revealed that I had a gene mutation called factor 5 leiden. According to a local geneticist, up to 80% of the population is a carrier. If not diagnosed, it leads to chemical pregnancy, miscarriage, still birth, and secondary infertility. Ultimately, this diagnosis would allow me to go on to hold and carry my pregnancies. Along with this diagnosis came hope.

Tip: If you have had even one miscarriage, or suspect chemical pregnancies, get tested for a blood clotting panel, especially factor 5 leiden.

In addition, I also had an undiagnosed thyroid issue causing my continuous bleeding from the surgery. Because of my blood loss, my red blood count was 2 points away from being fatal.

Diagnosed and back on the road to health with my now-fiancé, I knew that I still had some problems to solve. The endometriosis surgery had eliminated most (but not all) of my pain but not the torrential flow that became the norm. I sought out our town's only reproductive endocrinologist that specializes in infertility to get recommendations on next steps. He recommended my gynecologist perform a laparoscopic surgery to determine/remove any fibroids he could see.

The laparoscopic surgery was unsuccessful. My OB/GYN couldn't see a single fibroid to remove. Seeing my anguish, he let me know that there might be another type of fibroid surgery that could be done by the REI to be certain that I didn't have any fibroids. He explained that when looking into the uterus, the fibroids might be receding into the wall of the uterus. A saline infusion sonogram would allow the surgeon to see the fibroids better.

Bounced back to my REI, I scheduled the surgery as soon as I could. I was willing to do whatever it took to get to the bottom of my pain. When I woke up, I was shocked by the news the surgeon had for me.

Not only did he find that I DID, in fact, have fibroids, he removed so many that it looked like a handful of aquarium gravel. I was horrified because all that I could think about was whether or not each fibroid scar would be one less piece of real estate in my uterus but also thrilled because I was hopeful that this meant I would be pain-free.

Now, with the endo and fibroids gone, I *was sure* we were on a short path to parenthood. One month went by and then two. I was pain-free and having normal cycles now but more concerned than ever about the ticking clock and no pregnancy.

Now that my problems were cleared up, I started to question if something could be wrong with my husband. No one ever suggested my husband be tested for male factor infertility.

> TIP: Request as much testing up front as you can. Even if you have to pay out of pocket for it. Don't wait (for time, miscarriages, or failed IVF/IUI) to start procedures/testing. Don't wait to test your partner until issues with you are ruled out.

My husband got a glowing report on his swimmers, and we were back to the drawing board.

During our next two week wait, we decided to splurge and take a combined birthday/anniversary trip to Disney to relax and take a break from all thing's fertility-related (at least the painful ones). We ate a lot of good food, drank a lot of good wine, and then, at Epcot, got on the world's largest centrifuge (in the form of the ride Mission Space).

When we returned home, I went straight to acupuncture treatment. Afterward, Dr. H. and I decided to attend a chamber of commerce function. As we were walking around the different tables, she reached over to grab my hand and feel my pulse. She stopped dead in her tracks and turned to face me squarely, still gripping my wrist. "You're pregnant! and it's a boy!"

"What?!" I say, "I haven't even taken a pregnancy test." It was several more days of waiting before I was brave enough to confirm the prediction. We WERE pregnant and over the moon with excitement! It was my first positive pregnancy test ever.

Once the pregnancy was confirmed and the blood thinners on board to prevent a clot, we went about our business in the manner of any new and excited parents. I continued to work and, although monitored very closely, didn't have any scares, minus some spotting during an out-of-town business trip. It was a perfectly uneventful pregnancy.

We welcomed our first son after a 28-hour labor prevented him from being born on Christmas Day. I was 36.

After 15 months with a *super easy* baby, we were convinced that we were genius parents and ready to expand our family. We knew from the start that we wanted as many children as the Lord would allow us to have.

We returned to the same REI (in hindsight, I'm not sure why), and he had an even bleaker prognosis for us. After two and a half years, my blood work, including my AMH, was terrible. When he looked at my follicle count via ultrasound, he declared that I would need donor eggs in order to conceive. I think we were both stunned with disbelief.

My husband and I never even talked about using donor eggs as an option. Instead, we decided to drive an hour away for a second opinion. Unfortunately, this doctor wasn't any more optimistic about my outcome. He *did,* however, suggest that I take the blood thinners that I would need during pregnancy before we got a positive pregnancy test. He handed me a prescription and sent us on our way. It was Tuesday, and we were in our two week wait window.

Friday, I woke up feeling optimistic enough to take an early test. Much to my surprise, it was positive!!!! I couldn't believe my eyes. I rushed to the pharmacy to fill my prescription and schedule an ultrasound with my doctor.

While I was caring for our not quite two-year-old and waiting for the ultrasound, my husband noticed that I often referred to the pregnancy as "they" or "them." Hmm. That's weird, I thought. I wonder why I'm doing that? Both my husband and I had prophetic dreams about having twin girls.

Finally, it was ultrasound day, and we relayed our suspicions to the doctor. "Nope, just one baby here." We weren't disappointed and just blew it off. We were happily pregnant again.

I was very sick very early in the pregnancy. I had an ultrasound scheduled, but my husband stayed home (the only ultrasound he ever missed) with our son, who had the sniffles. The doctor placed the ultrasound wand on my stomach, and as the screen lit up, there were two "fried egg" images on the screen. It was the top of both my sons' heads. "That looks like twins!" I said. "It sure does!" he replied. Our prediction was correct.

Our twin boys were born at 39 weeks, 27 months after the birth of their big brother, one vaginally and one via c-section. I wouldn't change a thing about the outcome of our birth experience. Happy as a family of five, we struggled through our first year of twin life and then hit our stride the second year.

One morning, one of the boys woke me up. We had just returned from vacation, and my husband was gone on a business trip. The night before, I'd realized that I lost track of my period, and I reminded myself that when one of the boys woke in the morning, I would take a pregnancy test I had left over, "just in case." I peed on the stick, set it aside, and went to care for my son, almost forgetting on my way back to bed that I hadn't looked at it.

I was unconcerned, after all of our previous tracking, that this could be a "surprise" pregnancy. After all, I was 41. I flipped on the light and was STUNNED to see two dark lines staring back at me. We were pregnant! WOW. The birth would be the exact same spacing as the first two. Twenty-seven months.

The pregnancy was problematic from the start. First of all, it was the Friday before Labor Day weekend. I phoned the office as soon as they opened to make sure I got my blood thinner medicine before the weekend. It didn't happen. They closed at noon. It would be late the following week before they could see me.

Despite my panic, I tried to tell myself that it would be okay. I was wrong. By the time I was seen for my first appointment, they couldn't detect a heartbeat. They sent me to the hospital for a second detailed ultrasound, and I learned that I miscarried not one but two babies. We will always feel like that was our twin girls.

The miscarriage was devastating. Busy with the boys and convinced that another pregnancy was out of the question, we gave accidental pregnancy very little thought. Now, we were determined this miscarriage would not be how our story ended.

Months passed and then the year anniversary of the miscarriage. I was 42 and needed surgery to correct a severe diastasis rectus from the twin's pregnancy (combined, I carried over 12 pounds of baby) that left me looking five months pregnant on my size 4 frame.

We set a deadline of January 1st, 2015, to stop trying. I would be

43 that year and needed closure. I had given up hope. Seventeen months after the loss of our twins, and just two days before our "deadline," we got our positive pregnancy test!

After another uneventful pregnancy, I delivered, via unmedicated VBAC, our last son. It was truly a redemptive experience. We call him our 11th hour baby.

We welcomed our fourth son **SEVEN** years after medical professionals told us that we would not be able to conceive on our own or would need donor eggs. There are a lot of procedures/surgeries and details I was not able to include here due to space constraints. Some of these include massive changes in my diet, including switching to organic proteins, then organic veggies, then low/no processed foods. I eliminated soda from my diet, which is a killer to gut health (gut health is foundational to your hormones). I had a hysterosalpingography (HSG), which I believe helped "unblock" my tubes by proxy. There were two iron IV infusion treatments due to low ferritin (but normal iron levels). I outline all the steps that I believe helped me conceive and all that I've learned since then, in my course by the same name -- "Infertility Success." I'm determined to help as many women as I can get to the families of their dreams.

Also not mentioned, the emotional toll month after month of grieving as my period appeared and reappeared. Not to mention months of faking a smile and shrugging off intrusive questions to get through my job. When our oldest son was one, I went on hiatus from my very stressful sales job and, two months later, conceived our twins. It was a financial sacrifice that took us years of adjustments to recover from, but I 100% believe it contributed to their conception.

Only after the fact, and years later, did I realize that I had many, many chemical pregnancies. There were always the tell-tale signs and symptoms of pregnancy, and then I would get my cycle, and they faded away.

TIP: Don't discount the little things (coffee, toxins, dehydration, gut health, sleep, stress, exercise); all can dramatically affect the outcome of your procedure and getting pregnant on your own.

I'll leave you with this. If a doctor tells you **they** can't help you, it doesn't mean you can't get pregnant. I didn't get pregnant because I was special, but because I was willing to exhaust any and all obstacles to build the family of our dreams.

MORE TITLES AVAILABLE ON AMAZON

Infertility Success, Stories of Help and Hope for Your Journey
Infertility Success, **MORE** Stories of Help and Hope for Your Journey
Infertility Success, Stories of Faith and Miracles

TELL US WHAT YOU THINK

Dear Reader,

Thank you so much for investing your time in reading "Infertility Success to Postpartum Mess". Your support and interest mean the world to us the authors. I hope you found help in the journey and at least feel less alone. We wrote it for that very reason.

Your opinion matters a great deal to us and to other potential readers. If you could spare a few moments to leave a review on Amazon.com, it would be greatly appreciated. Your feedback not only helps other readers discover this book but also helps us grow and improve as authors.

If you're not sure what to write about, here are some guiding questions:

1. Which part of the book resonated with you the most and why?
2. Did the book inspire hope in you or provoke new thoughts? If so, how?
3. Would you recommend this book to others? Why or why not?

If you're sharing your thoughts on social media, please use the hashtags #BookTitleReview and #EricaHoke. It would be thrilling to see your thoughts in the wider world!

Before signing off, here's a little trivia for you: Writing "Infertility Success to Postpartum Mess " was born from some authors from Infertility Success, Stories of Help and Hope for Your Journey sharing how traumatic our postpartum motherhood journey was. We knew then and there that we had to shine a light on this dark place that no one talks about. We hope we have done just that for you.

If you feel inspired to share *your story* in a future project please reach out to me erica@ericahoke.com

Once again, thank you for your support and for being a part of this journey. Your feedback truly makes a difference.

Warm Regards, Erica Hoke

www.ingramcontent.com/pod-product-compliance
Lightning Source LLC
Chambersburg PA
CBHW071623040426
42452CB00009B/1456